T0193229

ESPECIALLY *to* THOSE WHO SUFFER

ESPECIALLY *to* THOSE WHO SUFFER

A Memoir of Truths and Miracles

Julija Rudolf

ESPECIALLY TO THOSE WHO SUFFER
A MEMOIR OF TRUTHS AND MIRACLES

iUniverse books may be ordered through booksellers or by contacting:

iUniverse
1663 Liberty Drive
Bloomington, IN 47403
www.iuniverse.com
1-800-Authors (1-800-288-4677)

Because of the dynamic nature of the Internet, any web addresses or links contained in this book may have changed since publication and may no longer be valid. The views expressed in this work are solely those of the author and do not necessarily reflect the views of the publisher, and the publisher hereby disclaims any responsibility for them.

Any people depicted in stock imagery provided by Getty Images are models, and such images are being used for illustrative purposes only. Certain stock imagery © Getty Images.

ISBN: 978-1-5320-8488-1 (sc)
ISBN: 978-1-5320-8490-4 (hc)
ISBN: 978-1-5320-8489-8 (e)

Library of Congress Control Number: 2020906941

Print information available on the last page.

iUniverse rev. date: 04/24/2020

DEDICATION

I dedicate my memoir to my friends and acquaintances, to all those who have planted the seeds for growth in my soul.

I dedicate my lifelong endeavor to my doctors, therapists, and those who have provided counsel in order for my mind to flourish.

I dedicate my life's work to all of the angels, who are my wonderful family—especially to my dear brother and gentle sister who suffered for my sake.

I dedicate this book, *Especially to Those Who Suffer*, to my lifelong companion, artist, and car enthusiast—my husband.

And, in a very special way, I dedicate my accomplishment of writing a book—of achieving happiness and peace of mind within the pages of it—to you, mom and dad. To you, I give my unconditional love, and for you, I have been named!

INTRODUCTION

I fondly remember Brad, my psychologist, in 2005. He was one of many helpers who led me to self-awareness, which led to peace of mind. Brad used hypnosis to unravel the mysteries of my subconscious. His beautiful parables eased the constant anxiety I suffered for most of my life. He told me a fable once while I was in a deep hypnotic sleep that genuinely describes who I am.

"Julija," he began, "you are like a little seed that blew in the wind until finally resting on rocky soil. The sun shone on you, and the rains quenched your thirst. Against all the odds, you took root."

Entranced, I felt Brad's words as he continued. "Your roots took hold in the sparse soil of a tiny crevice and became stronger and stronger. Finally, one day, your bloom burst open into the most beautiful flower. Julija, you are that flower!" With all the wonderful stories Brad told, this is my favorite. It reflects my life.

I journal and have hundreds of hand-worked leather books. I freely open these up to you. My only desire in exposing my secrets is for you to "bloom" as I did.

My story begins in 1986. I will cover a sampling of significant events from journal entries I made throughout the passing years. All the names I used, including my pen name, are fictitious. I wish to protect my privacy and that of my family. May you find your happiness and freedom from suffering.

PART I

THE WORKING YEARS

CHAPTER 1

The Good Friday Joke

April 1, 1986

It was an ordinary Tuesday morning at A Corp when I filled my TR6 coffee mug to the brim with my morning wake-me-up. Our director, Elwood, was already in Steve, my supervisor's office, with his cup of coffee. Yes, everything was quite normal.

Elwood was the "big" boss of the Credit and Accounts Receivable Departments at A Corp. He was Steve's immediate boss, and since Steve was my supervisor, Elwood was my high-muck-a-muck, as my dear friend Elizabeth would say. Elwood had a peculiar personality. For instance, his favorite topic was Penn State football. He followed every single game and newscast that involved them or their famous coach. You would think that he was their biggest fan. However, he was gleeful when they lost a game. He hated everything about Penn State. I sat in silence during these tirades even though I was taking part-time courses at Penn State, and was a fan. He knew that, and I knew my place.

It was the Tuesday after Easter Sunday, so I had a late start to my work week since I took off Easter Monday as usual. Oh, it was a grand Easter that year. I wore my new Halston royal blue and ivory silk suit for church. But the coup d'état was the royal blue straw hat that topped my ensemble. I felt like a British royal. Maybe even Princess Di. Alas, I was back in the real world in my tiny cubicle outside of Steve's office.

I settled in when Steve summoned me loudly, "Oh, Juljia, come in here!"

I immediately "obeyed" my boss. Steve and I had worked together since 1978. He was difficult to work for. He always talked about his wife, who immigrated to this country with her family when she was six years old. He sounded quite proud of her Italian heritage. Last Christmas, I had given him an Italian Christmas album.

He opened the present and announced in disgust, "My wife is Italian, not me. This is for her!"

He didn't talk to me for three days! He eventually got over it, but, per his request, that was the last time we exchanged Christmas presents. Now I stood before Elwood and Steve. *What could he possibly want?*

"Elwood, do you know what Julia did? Do YOU know what she did?"

Suddenly, the heat of fear flowed through my body. I knew what he was going to say. I fingered the folds of my dress like a nervous child.

No, please don't tell him! He doesn't like me as it is! I tried to run out of his office.

"Stay, Julija! Stay!" Steve commanded.

I froze in place.

But Steve continued, "Julija called Paul and gave him the answer to our riddle on Friday!"

Oh, my God! He knew! He must have waited all weekend to "get" me. My mind whirled back to Friday, Good Friday. *Elwood and Steve were going to bully Paul once again, and, this time, I wasn't going to let it happen.*

Paul was an account manager who reported directly to Steve. His office was next to Steve, and my cubbyhole faced both of their offices.

Paul was a happy-go-lucky sort who all the ladies liked. Diane made him her famous shoofly pie and Cindy her delicious sugar cookies. Paul was an avid Penn State fan, and on his credenza, he proudly displayed all his memorabilia, along with a picture of his adorable wife. Elwood and Steve were not that popular with the women in our department. Elwood and Steve were so jealous of Paul. It became a sport to them to put him down in their sick sort of way. *But, not this time.*

On that past Good Friday, March 28, 1986, I heard Elwood plotting with Steve to tell Paul a riddle that "he will never get right." *Honest to God!* Earlier in the week, Elwood and his new secretary, who was even more vindictive than he was, hung a sign they made that read, "DUMMY" under Paul's nameplate. Now they were going to try to make a fool out of him again.

Like devious school bullies, they waited for Paul to return to his office so that they could pounce on him with their ridiculous riddle. I was sick of it and, for once, I was going to do something about it. And I did. Amid their sick joke, I silently called Paul's telephone extension and gave him the riddle's answer. It was done.

Currently, following a beautiful Easter weekend, I was frozen in place in Steve's office. I was petrified. Something happened to my mind that day. I don't remember what Elwood said or did. I don't even remember leaving Steve's office. I walked in a trance all day. *Why did he do that to me?* I thought Steve, who was my age, was my friend. I even washed his coffee cup for him every day, and I gave him an azalea plant for Easter.

CHAPTER 2

The Falling Out

April 15, 1986

A couple of weeks after the infamous "joke" incident in Accounts Receivable, Steve and Elwood were at it again. This time they were in Paul's office with the door closed: a sure sign of trouble! *Poor Paul!* He sat there red-faced listening to their grim antics. I was not surprised when Paul called me into his office after the duo were out of sight.

"Jules, they wrote me up but would not tell me why or what I did wrong."

"Did you ask why?"

"Yes," he glumly replied, "they would not tell me."

How can a reasonable person discipline an employee and not tell them what they did wrong? Then I remembered I had heard earlier in the week that Trudy, a junior cash clerk who was laid off months ago, ran into Mr. Miner, a company executive, Elwood's boss, and a friend of Trudy's family. Mr. Miner had likely sent her to Elwood to get her job back.

I put two and two together here. Trudy wanted her job back, and Elwood and Steve didn't like her. They didn't want her back. After all, isn't that why they laid her off in the first place? Well, Paul got along quite well with Trudy, as he did everyone. It was no secret that he just talked to her when she called our office this week.

"Paul, did you tell Trudy they were hiring again?"

"No," was his immediate response.

I said no more than that to him. I was afraid to blame Mr. Miner. He was an executive, and I was scared of him. The following days at the office were horrible for me! I sat facing two men who were not on speaking terms anymore!

Paul would call out to me, "Jules, do you want to go to Joe's Tavern for a spaghetti lunch today?" *God, tell me, how was I possibly going to appease both?* I had too much anxiety to sit where I did! Then there was Elwood, whose large corner office was right next to Steve. He heard all of this transpire, and he was still pissy because of the joke incident. Plus, there was Elwood's weird secretary, Sheila. She was an unhappy, anorexic young lady. She showed her dysfunction repeatedly. She and Elwood would get their heads together and make derogatory remarks about everyone and anyone. I especially despised their not-so-nice dealings with the special needs mail clerk, Larry. Sheila sat there and flirted with Larry when he delivered the mail.

Then, after he went on his way, Elwood would quip to her, "You want him, don't you?" They thought it was hilarious! It makes me angry to remember it. It was sick.

That did not stop me from trying to please Sheila; after all, I had to work with her. One time, while shopping, I ran across a beautiful parrot brooch on sale. Sheila had parrots, and she loved birds. I bought it for her and was anxious to present her with the gift. But my thoughtfulness did not please her. It had the extreme opposite effect on her. She sat there with a scowl on her face. When I looked up, Elwood was seated at his desk, staring at me with the same expression. The whole experience made me extremely self-conscious. It wouldn't be long until I heard insulting comments that, I believed, were directed at me too. God.

CHAPTER 3

The Social Phobia Exposed

April 22, 1986

Alas, the tension became too high for me. I realized it today when Sheila came up to my desk.

"I need you to add a $10,000 machine rental charge to A Corp's Canada account," directed Sheila.

She expected me to pull out my manual bookkeeping index card as she stood by my desk to make sure I completed her request. But something suddenly clicked in my mind. A familiar heat swept through my body. My hands trembled. I no longer had control of my hands. I could not do it. God, I could not pull out that file. My mind focused only on how I was going to hide my phobia from this woman.

As I responded to her request with, "I'll get it later," I saw the surprised, almost satisfied look on her face.

She saw my hands shaking. God.

I have a social phobia that has plagued me since 1969. It began when I was a junior in high school. I remember my days at the soda fountain with Shatz, my high school sweetheart. I couldn't drink the lime soda the clerk put in front of me. Instead of picking the glass up for the straw to meet my lips, I awkwardly bent down to sip the beverage. The anxiety disorder became worse as time went by. I constantly ruminated about how I would hide it from people when I had to use my hands in public. It dictated everything in my life, especially my occupation.

My secret was exposed after working in Accounts Receivable for eight years. There would be no turning back for me now! I had to find a way to quell office tension. I had to make peace between Steve and Paul.

With great determination, I pulled Paul aside and opined, "Paul, you have to try to talk to Steve. Just talk to him. Maybe you can clear this mess up."

But I could tell that Paul didn't believe that Steve would tell him anything when he responded, "I tried Jules."

Well, I wasn't getting anywhere with Paul. There was only one recourse. I had to talk to Steve about it.

I had a plan and put it into action at five o'clock when everyone was leaving the office for the evening. I walked out to the parking lot with Steve instead of with Michelle and Arlene as I usually did. I was uncomfortable, and seeing that Steve only looked straight ahead, he must have been too.

There was no other option but to blurt out my thoughts, "Steve," I began, "You have to talk to Paul. He didn't do what you think he did."

Then with a deep breath, "I know who did, but I'm not going to say. You can clear this up. Just talk to him."

And then nothing—nothing!

CHAPTER 4

It Would Only Snowball

April 25, 1986

I realized things were way out of control. The office walls were not soundproof. *Didn't they know I could hear everything said in Steve's office from my desk?*

I overheard Elwood say to Steve, "She's probably having an affair with Paul!"

Then after devious laughter between the duo, "She's probably pregnant from him!"

Steve had repeated my conversation with him to Elwood. I was stunned. Elwood looked at me through the glass. I'm sure my face showed my horror. I wanted to cry. I lost a friend. At least, I thought Steve and I were friends. I used to say he was my "umbrella," shielding me from usual office intrigues. But Steve believed I was taking Paul's side of their dispute. I knew that I lost the battle, and it would only snowball from there.

After supper, Bill, my husband since 1976, went to the local "watering hole" as he did every night. I lay in bed, hugging my Bible to my chest and cried.

I called out for my daddy, who died three years earlier.

"Dad!" I screamed out to the heavens imagining the sound waves traveling through space, "I lost my friend. I lost my friend!"

Tears fell onto the burgundy leather cover of the "good book," and I sobbed myself to sleep.

April 28, 1986

I can tell you now that anyone who suffers from crippling phobias and panic attacks is stronger than they believe. At least, I never was one to give up. I was of stubborn Eastern European descent. Not to stereotype, but I saw the strength of my parents.

It had not been a good weekend for me. I was dizzy with neurosis for two days. I wanted them to stop talking about me. I had a plan to stop them from ridiculing me. I mustered up the courage and went into Steve's office. He was sitting at his desk reading the *Wall Street Journal* as I sat down in the chair right next to him.

"On Friday, I heard you and Elwood saying that I was having an affair and was probably pregnant from Paul," I announced with a trembling voice.

He didn't even look surprised at my blunt statement and responded, "We were just joking as we do about everybody."

Stunned by his insensitive response, I said no more. So, the "snowball" began to roll. The ridiculing by Steve, Elwood, and Sheila didn't end. It only got worse.

God, didn't they know? Didn't they know how much it hurt me? Oh, daddy, daddy, I can't forget how they hurt me. I wept over my life of suffering. *Jesus, I walked the passion all my life. Somehow, I kept going. God, how did I keep going?*

CHAPTER 5

Blood in the Trachea

May 1983

So many things happened in the eighties before the ill-fated joke at A Corp. One warm spring evening, I heard the tingle of the little Liberty Bell we kept at the side of dad's bed. He was calling me. It was hard to see my daddy completely childlike because that dreaded cancer was stealing the essence of this steelworker's body. After the experimental surgery he went through in October 1982, he couldn't speak, eat, or breathe. We fed him through a tube placed in his shoulder that led to his stomach, and he had a trachea to breathe. He resorted to the notes he scribbled with calloused hands to communicate.

That day, he handed me a scribbled paper, "Where do we go from here?"

I confess that I couldn't always figure out what he was "saying." *Was it cancer in his brain, or was that the drug cocktail we were administering through the tube?* That evening, he didn't have to write me a note. I heard the rattle in his chest. I instinctively knew that he needed his trachea suctioned out by the monster machine stationed at the side of his bed. That week, my sister Catherine and I were trying to keep dad at home. It was back and forth between there and my home. Catherine and I both slept on the parlor floor so that we could hear the tiny bell rang. That day,

Hospice had come, and so had Father Leonard, dad's priest friend from St. Margaret's Church, to give him Last Rites.

The whirling motor of the machine broke the silence with a gurgle as I inserted the suction tube into the hole in dad's throat. If someone had told me that I would be suctioning out a trachea, I would have told him that I couldn't do it. It was indeed instinctual to know when to pull that tube out. Everything appeared normal at first.

But then, I was startled, *there's blood in the trachea!*

The breath of fear rushed through my body. The kind nurse at the local medical center who had instructed us how to use the machine told us to watch for signs of trauma such as blood in the trachea.

"That is when you call the hospital," she stated.

On the verge of panic, I ran to the telephone in the dining room; I couldn't think. *Where is that number?* Somehow, I managed to place the call to the medical center.

My voice quivered as the Emergency Room doctor came to the phone after what seemed like an eternity.

"I'm bringing my father in. He has blood in his trachea."

The doctor coldly responded, "You can't bring him in here for everything."

And so, I resigned myself to watch and wait.

But the wait took a turn for the worse. Soon after my desperate call for help, blood trickled from the corner of dad's mouth. Suddenly, large clots came up into his mouth. Without a minute to lose, I reached in and pulled clots as large as lemons from his mouth with my hands. I kept pulling out the balls of blood. *Oh, God.* They kept coming out. I feared he was drowning in his own blood. Catherine wasn't home. Mom was there, but she wasn't good with emergencies. When I felt it was safe, I rushed out to call for an ambulance.

Catherine came home about the same time the ambulance arrived. I needed her support. I was a shaking mess inside, but I had no choice. Thank God the paramedics allowed me to ride with daddy. I was determined not to leave his side. *He's dying; he's dying,* circled my mind as I positioned my body across his chest to keep him stable on the litter. He must have believed that as well. He took off his old Timex watch that he treasured and gave it to me. *God, dad. God, it hurts.*

If that damn arrogant doctor from the medical center had agreed to see dad when I called him, I wouldn't have experienced this trauma alone. I was already angry at what that medical center did to my dad in October 1982. They performed experimental surgery on him prolonging and worsening his suffering, which inevitably led to his death.

After a lengthy wait, the surgeon entered the waiting area, "We were able to stop the bleeding and are moving him to a room now."

That wasn't going to be the end of this horrible place. A couple of days later, while I sat next to my father's bed, a social worker came into his hospital room.

"There is nothing more we can do for him," she stated, "You have to make arrangements to put him in a nursing facility."

Oh God, what were we going to do? Our family didn't have that kind of money, and mom couldn't lose the house. She worked too hard to keep it when dad had his car accident in 1953. I knew he would not want that for her.

Once home, I sat on the stool in our bathroom and wailed in grief, "They did this to my dad, and now they don't even want him."

God Almighty. God Almighty.

I cried from the depths of my soul. *They were throwing my dad out. Couldn't they let him die in peace? Look what they did to this man, and now they don't want him!*

The next day we had to move fast. Catherine and I debated what to do. It was evident to us that we could no longer take care of dad at home. He needed medical care. Then I got the idea. Dad was a World War II veteran.

"Let's see if we can put dad in the Veteran's Administration Hospital," I said to Catherine and Mike, our brother.

Mike, is the middle child, being five years younger than myself and five years older than Catherine. He is married to Anna and is a welder by trade. He thought it was a good idea, but Catherine wanted to visit there first to "check it out."

I was comfortable with the veteran's hospital. I remembered going there as a child. Dad was in and out of that hospital for years when he pulverized his leg in the car accident. When I was two years old, Mom and I would take the bus to visit him there.

I would stand outside, and mom instructed me, "Wave to your dad," as he appeared in the window several floors up. *God Almighty.*

Catherine finally agreed to place dad in the VA Hospital, and more importantly, they accepted my father there. It wasn't long until mom, Catherine, Mike and I surrounded dad's bed in that hospital ward. After dad wrote out, "Where?" I knew my answer gave him peace to know he was in the VA. He was concerned about mom losing the house.

Since the hospital was so far away, we only visited him every other day. I have a long-distance driving phobia, and mom didn't drive, so we relied on Catherine and Mike. It was only about a week after dad was placed there, May 15, 1983, when the nurse stopped Catherine and I as we exited the elevator on dad's floor.

"I'm sorry, but your father was moved to another room. He took a turn for the worse," she went on, "he's in a coma."

The floor nurse led Catherine and I to a spacious room with green flowered curtains. She had placed her radio by the side of dad's bed to play country music for him. *How did she know that was his favorite?* I was numb inside. *God, I couldn't feel anymore.* I had too much on my plate. Bill recently had a DUI and wrecked my TR6. It only had liability insurance, and I was without a car. *Was he going to jail?* I was on the phone with crisis intervention all night while Bill slept it off. *God, how much pain can a person endure?*

Catherine and I sat on the chairs by dad's bed, and we talked to each other for what seemed like a long time. Only about fifteen minutes had passed when suddenly, dad sat straight up. He had heard Catherine and me! He gave us a beautiful smile and waved to us. My dad. My daddy. He wanted to get out of bed, but we assured him that he was okay and bade him lie back down. And that was it. He fell back into that deep sleep. When it was time for us to leave, I knew in my heart that would be the last time I saw my beloved father. Merrilee Rush was singing, "Angel of the Morning" on the radio. I listened to the words intently, "Just touch my cheek before you leave me." I asked my sister to wait until the song was over. I kissed my dad goodbye, and it was done. That was the last time I saw my father.

On the morning of May 17, 1983, mom's voice on the telephone reported, "Dad died." The days following the loss of my father—the funeral—were a blur to me. Now, the flag that covered his coffin is in a place of honor on my fireplace mantle.

CHAPTER 6

The Door

March 16, 1986

The years after dad's death moved on, and I, maybe more than anyone, missed his presence at Catherine's wedding. My sister was stunning in her unique 1940's style white satin dress as Mike walked her down the aisle. I saw the admiration on David, her fiancé's face, as he stood at the altar to take her extended hand. Sadly, my dad didn't get to see his lovely redheaded daughter on her special day.

During the year leading up to the wedding, I helped Catherine plan and execute the marvelous affair we called "Putting on the Ritz." I took on the role of surrogate mother to her. A year after dad died, mom sank into major depression. It was extremely hard dealing with this woman who kept calling me for help but refused medical treatment.

The day after the wedding, I cautiously traversed the highway to the Catholic Cemetery, which, to my disdain, was outside of my "safe" driving range. I was going to honor my father with the five white roses I carried down the aisle in church the day before. I would leave them with pure love on his headstone.

It was late in the afternoon when I reached my destination. *I wouldn't want to be here any later in the day.* I walked up the hilltop to dad's grave. Suddenly, time stopped. It was like I stepped through a portal and was in another dimension. My physical sight turned inward. It was mystical. For an instant, I felt like I could ask anything about the future and know the answer. Stunned, I didn't ask anything, at least, not right away.

Then, just as the door was about to close, I sensed a voice in my mind tell me, "You will not die of breast cancer."

My fibrocystic breast disease was a constant source of anxiety for me. I was just at the surgeon who performed a cyst aspiration biopsy the week before.

After a slight hesitation, I finally did ask my question, "Then how will I die?"

But it was too late, and the door closed like it opened. A wave of peace took the place of the anxiety. All I knew was that something I couldn't explain had happened to me. I placed the flowers on dad's tombstone and headed home. It was getting late.

CHAPTER 7

The Psychiatrist

May 9, 1986

I am in a very bad way today. All the planning for Catherine's wedding is over, and I am tired, very tired. However, Elwood and Steve were not letting up with their derogatory comments, and I could no longer hide my phobias. I felt them watching me all the time, especially Elwood. They were in Steve's office talking about me again, and I had to sit at my desk and listen to them.

"Look at her face," Elwood said, "Look at it now!"

Well, you tell me! How am I supposed to look? I can hear you in that office making fun of me. Don't you think I would have a peculiar look on my face? I knew what I had to do. When I quit smoking for three months once before, the phobias weren't as bad. I was calmer. I must quit now before the shaking propels out of control. I pitched my leftover cigarettes. *Tomorrow would be a new day full of hope.*

May 10, 1986

Saturday morning arrived, and I was in a horrible mental fog. All I could think of was smoking. The quit-smoke neurosis ran through me. It paralleled the experience I had as a child when I had my teeth pulled. Back then, the nurse circled round and round, and I was stuck within the ether mask on my face. My nerves couldn't sustain my anxiety. *I need a cigarette.*

Bill hadn't come home the night before until two in the morning. I sat by the window most of the night watching for his truck to turn into our driveway. *What kind of trouble will he get into tonight?* I needed a cigarette then, but it was too late. I had already thrown them away. God, I would have pulled them out of the garbage, but I ran water over them to avoid caving in and doing that very thing. I cleaned out ashtrays too, or I would have resorted to relighting butts.

That's it! I'm going to Turkey Hill (the local convenience store)! I have a good reason to smoke today. After all, I was up half the night. I'll quit tomorrow. I tried to appease myself. I was in the store parking lot, anticipating relief as my fingers fumbled to open the just-purchased pack of cigarettes. Finally, after a deep inhalation, the nicotine rushed to my brain, and I reached the temporary high that I so needed.

At last, the neurosis resolved, but only for a minute. Then, guilt set in. God, the guilt was intense. All I could think of was killing myself. I couldn't quit the habit.

God, I need to do something. Anything. I can't take it anymore; the pain is too great. I must quit smoking. Ten years before, I had looked up a psychiatrist to help me with the phobias. Bill said that I didn't need one back then, and unfortunately, I had listened to him. As soon as I was in the door, I pulled out the telephone directory to see if that doctor was still practicing. I searched under hypnosis. The psychiatrist had used hypnosis as part of his therapy. *God, if I could just quit smoking with hypnosis, I wouldn't get the shaking hands or the social phobia I've had since I was in my teens.* I knew it helped once before in one of my short-lived "quit" attempts. This morning's failed attempt left me wanting to hurt myself. I was buried in the quit-smoking neurosis. I couldn't take it anymore. It has been two months since "the joke" at A Corp and the situation there was not good. My hands were shaking to the point where I couldn't hide it anymore.

Since it was a Saturday, I didn't expect to hear anything but a recording on Dr. Andrews' answering system. I didn't care. I needed to hear it, to know I might get help. Much to my surprise, the doctor answered the telephone himself.

"Are you in danger of hurting yourself?" he inquired.

"No," I said. *Not anymore, anyway!* After my reassurances to him, we set up my appointment for the next Saturday.

May 17, 1986

I had my appointment with Dr. Andrews, a distinguished, white-haired physician. I was quite nervous as I surveyed his bookshelf lined office in the Medical Arts Building. On a bookshelf, He had books on philosophy and one on Edgar Cayce. He also had a picture of himself with his friend, who was a priest. My dad had a friend who was a priest. During World War II, dad was a chaplain's assistant. Perhaps that was why he was always so dedicated to the Catholic faith. That was probably why I was comfortable opening up to Dr. Andrews.

"I've had anxiety all of my life," I began. "I can no longer go to communion at Mass. I can't walk down the aisle. I'm too phobic of the people in the church," I told him.

He revealed, "I'm Catholic, too!"

We went on and on, talking for the whole hour. He said that my fondness for veterans was my maternal instinct, and of course, we talked about my addiction to tobacco. Well, that was all it took for a bond to develop between us. Since my dad instilled my religious convictions in me as a child, Dr. Andrews immediately became a father figure to me. On the drive home, I felt hope for the first time in quite a while.

CHAPTER 8

Enveloped in Darkness

I had sessions with Dr. Andrews once a month. It was so easy for me to sink into a hypnotic trance. I trusted him right away. The doctor told me that I had a gift for hypnosis.

However, my first hypnotic trance with him was frightening. He guided me into a deep meditative state with his soft-spoken words. I felt myself floating above the trees, guided by the wind.

"Just allow whatever will help you now to surface," he directed.

I didn't know what to expect, but suddenly, I developed rapid eye movement. And then I was enveloped in darkness, a bottomless dark pit! A fear I had never met overcame me. My body muscles tensed up in fright, and I wanted to scream at the top of my lungs. God, I just wanted to scream! But there was a part of me who heard the waiting room door open, and I knew someone was sitting out there. I could not make a sound.

My session with Dr. Andrews was about to end, and he began to speak of the "quit smoking" issue. That was my main goal.

I did not tell him about the darkness and the fright I experienced in the trance. I certainly was perplexed by it, though. *What was the intense fear of the dark? What did this trance mean?*

We set up my next appointment for the following month and said our goodbyes. It gave me something to think about until the next month. Little did I know those subsequent hypnosis sessions with him were to get even more intense as the years passed. In particular, the saga of a young French girl whose life I recalled in the trance. I named her Marie Antoinette Chambre. *Was she me in a past life? Or was her story an analogy of my own life?* More about her later.

CHAPTER 9

He Was Light

June 14, 1986

It was a "special" Saturday once again. I had an appointment with my friend, the doctor. Also, that day, I had received the results of the mammogram from earlier in the week. I had had cyst aspirations since 1978. Fortunately, the results of the mammogram were good once again. But my pre-hypnosis discussion with Dr. Andrews usually contributed to what would come up in a trance. That day, breast cancer was on my mind. So, I told the doctor of my experience on March 16, 1986, in the cemetery with the "voice," saying, "You will not die of breast cancer."

It was the end of our conversation and time to begin my hypnotic trance.

Seated in the black recliner at the side of Dr. Andrews' desk, he instructed, "Allow what will help you to deal with where you are right now to come up."

I went into a deep trance, and, as usual, my rapid eye movement signaled that a story was about to unfold.

"It's opening!" I cried as my outstretched arms acted out a portal opening.

I never knew what story was going to come up in my trance. But I was glad when I realized that I was going to tell the cemetery story.

I was quite taken back when:

"Dad, dad!!" I cried. He was there. It was my dad!

I sobbed with joy as he appeared on the other side. I was with him. The only way I could describe the miracle was that I felt his essence-like energy. My hands were acting out how I contacted him by moving through and around him. *It was him! It was him!*

"I missed you so much!" I cried out with love and happiness to somehow be reunited with him again after so long.

Dad was talking to me. I felt myself listening to him. It was as if I could not consciously know what he was saying. I *felt* like he was telling me of things to come in my subconscious mind. Then, I sensed he was leaving.

"Don't leave me!" Tears streamed down my cheeks.

"Please don't leave me," I begged my father.

"You will be happy!" I heard him say in my mind.

Again, I motioned with my hands; this time, the portal was closing.

"It's closing," I was sad.

There was one last message to me. "You will not die of breast cancer." He declared.

"Then how will I die?" I finally asked, but it was too late. The door had closed.

"Don't tell anyone," I told myself out loud.

"They'll think I'm crazy!" My head sank to my shoulder as dad's departure left me fatigued and saddened.

After the hypnosis session and still seated in the recliner, Dr. Andrews asked me, "What did your dad look like?"

"He was light. But not light as you would know it." I think the doctor understood.

My dad had been with me again at that moment. I felt him. It's hard to explain, but I knew it was him immediately when the door opened. I cried tears of joy for him. I got to tell my daddy how much I missed him. Even so, I could not wrap my head around death. I don't understand my God. My mind was troubled despite this miraculous experience.

CHAPTER 10

A Downhill Spiral

1987

Thank God for the hypnosis sessions with Dr. Andrews. Every month I had a new story to reveal to him, and more importantly, to myself. Hypnosis became my outlet for dealing with the significant stress of A Corp. It was terrible there, and I had no idea that it was about to get worse.

It was a hectic end of the month, and the Accounts Receivable reconciliation had to be completed by the five o'clock deadline. I had a problem reconciling the statement balance for the Japan account. *God, that's all I need, an international incident.* My chest tightened and pressure built in my head. But I persevered because I loved that job. I am excellent with numbers. It is intuitive to me to find the answers to a problem. Also, it is incredible to talk to and correspond with the twenty-five foreign subsidiaries of A Corp. When the holidays arrived, my entire refrigerator was wallpapered with greeting cards from those countries.

For the tenth time that day, Sheila's telephone rang. I dropped everything, jumped up, ran over to her desk, and answered the phone. Marsha walked by me on the way back to my cubicle.

"How much time does she get off anyway?" she questioned sarcastically.

Sheila got ten days of vacation, like most others. But it was nothing new for her to leave whenever she wanted. It was summer, and every sunny afternoon, she was out, and I had to take up the slack! *I'm going to ask Steve what's going on.* He was another one who was never there. I answered his phone, and half the time, I could not say when he would be in again for a return call. My nerves were shot.

"Steve, why is Sheila always out? It's not just me who notices it. All the girls make comments when they pass by."

"I don't know. Ask Elwood," he replied flatly.

I did. Little did I know that was the beginning of the end for me. Oh, he told me, alright. He gave her twenty-eight day's comp time for cleaning out the file drawer folders at her home! We were in a time of austerity at A Corp with absolutely no overtime to be issued, and he gave her comp time! And to clean files? But it didn't end there.

A couple of days later, Elwood's boss called him to the office at the executive building. When he returned to our office, he was in a mighty foul mood. He did not have a good meeting with his bosses. *I wonder if he was written up.* I felt the tension in the air! From what I had heard coming from Elwood's office, it was the comp time that got him in trouble. To my horror, Elwood believed I was "telling" a corporate officer on him!

"Don't tell that skinny bitch anything!" he yelled to Steve.

I froze.

"There will be an exit. There will be an exit!" he exclaimed loudly.

I was horrified that he wanted me to hear. *I didn't do it!* I told my two close friends about the comp time, but no one else.

It became a downhill spiral for me in the office. The terrible trio, Elwood, Steve, and Sheila began to stand around my desk and whisper. It was so frequent that I kept track of the times of day they congregated around me. Then, they ridiculed everything they heard me say. I said and did nothing. I sat there, mortified.

As time went on, the terrible trio cut me off from essential information involving my work. For instance, they automated my card accounting system and told me nothing about it. Sheila, Elwood, and Steve worked with the Systems Department on the transition.

I didn't find out about it until the day I answered Steve's phone, and a Systems Analyst asked, "How does it feel to be automated?"

I was so stunned that I couldn't answer him. *God, it's my job!* They were taking my work away from me. I remembered back to the day I tried to make peace between Steve and Paul; God, I was so right when I suspected it was snowballing. That snowball was growing larger and larger. I was powerless, and my phobias intensified.

CHAPTER 11

The Medjugorje Vision

1988

It was the day that Steve called me into his office to change his adding machine tape that I knew I needed a miracle to survive at work. Steve was seated at his desk when I entered the office. Suddenly, fear welled up like a volcanic eruption in my mind. *Why didn't I wait until he wasn't there!* I was frantic. But it was too late. The phobia, I had known it was going to strike, and, sure enough, it did. My hands shook uncontrollably as my fingers tried to install the paper roll. *Oh my God,* Steve was watching me.

But he showed his humanity that day when he said, "That's okay. I'll do it."

I now realize that his bullying was a fear of getting on Elwood, his boss's "bad side." But it didn't have to be that way.

Work was sheer torture for me. I needed a miracle, and I knew where to go for it. At mom's weekly Sunday chicken dinner, I read a small ad that a local travel agency had placed in the newspaper. It announced a pilgrimage to an Eastern European village called Medjugorje, which is near the border of Croatia. I had heard of the miracles of healing occurring in this little village in Bosnia and Herzegovina through the Catholic church, where Bill and I were members. I believed in the apparitions of the Blessed Mother to the children of the village. After everything I had been through, I still believed in miracles. Surely there would be one for me there.

That Sunday, I queried, "Mom, do you want to go to Europe with me?"

That was all it took. She was as excited to go as I was!

The trip was that fall, and it was already August! We worked with the travel agency to obtain the necessary visas, passports, and travel tickets. Of course, I had to buy a new wardrobe to take with me! Before we knew it, October 10, 1988, finally arrived; and Bill saw mom and I off for our limousine ride to New York City.

All was going well with the exception that I could not sleep for the long airplane ride overseas. I peered out of the small round plane window almost the whole eleven-hour trip. I witnessed the dark of night turn into daylight as we traveled through six time zones. But seeing the tops of the amazing Alps was most impressive. After remaining awake for so long, I finally rested when we reached our first leg of the trip, the fairytale town of Dubrovnik.

After much-needed sleep in our beautiful suite facing the Adriatic Sea, morning arrived. That day we went to tour the Old Town of Dubrovnik. There, mom and I visited exquisite churches with elaborately decorated facades, as well as historic public buildings. The shopping was fantastic. I went through two rolls of film in that beautiful medieval city. Too soon, it was time to board a bus for the trip to Medjugorje.

The bus traversed narrow winding roads, and I kept snapping pictures of all the fantastic landmarks along the way. Even the haystacks fascinated me, along with the reams of tobacco drying in barns. The driver played a cassette of religious music, which added to the ambiance of our pilgrimage. I finally spotted it on the top of a mountain, a large concrete cross for all to see. It was the "Hill of the Cross" called Krizevac. We had arrived at Medjugorje!

After collecting our baggage from the storage area at the bottom of the bus, we met the family who would host us during our stay in the village. There were two homes that the family provided for our small tour group. The accommodations were simple, and we shared a community bathroom, but the people who hosted us were very kind. They met all our needs with their lunches of bread and cheeses and evening dinners of fish and poultry.

On our first evening there, we walked a narrow-wooded pathway, a shortcut as pointed out to us by our hosts, to Saint James Church. Sure enough, there it was. The building with tall twin-steeples appeared oversized for such a tiny village. Almost like when it was built long ago, it was intended to be the center of the miraculous happenings going on since 1981. My first feeling as I entered the courtyard in front of the church was the presence of evil. *Why? Why do I feel that?* There was a grouping of candles that flickered in the darkness. I spotted a bonfire at the top of Cross Mountain. There were so many people around singing and praying. People! It was eerie to me.

My strange first impression vanished as mom, and I eagerly went into St. James Church for the English evening mass. It was packed with people, and we stood off to one side of the aisle. There were people everywhere, and some were sitting on the floor. As I had told Dr. Andrews, I could not receive communion because of my devastating phobias. The phobias expanded to the point where I couldn't stand in line anywhere, even to check out at a store or cash a check at the bank. I certainly couldn't walk to the front of a church without feeling the doom of a severe panic attack. My heart would race to the point that I felt faint. That night, in the church, the neurosis of how to maneuver receiving the host reared its ugly head. But I was more determined to take communion at that mass than to care if my damn hands shook. Relief unburdened my mind when the priest came up to us to give us the host. The worry of standing in line and facing my anxiety diminished, and I took communion in my hands. They didn't shake! I was elated to receive the host after years of abstaining.

That is a smidgen of what happened upon arrival at that village. What happened on our third visit to St. James Church was forever instilled in my mind. It was Thursday, October thirteenth, and, once again, mom and I went through the narrow pathway that led to the church. People packed the church, and there wasn't even standing room inside the doorway. Mom and I stood outside out front with a canopy of stars overhead on that pleasant evening. It was 6:30 PM. A special time in the church was soon at hand. The Blessed Mother was to appear to the children of the village once again. We watched flashes of camera bulbs light up the church windows. People tried to capture a supernatural sign on their photos.

I silently prayed. As I peered up into the sky between the steeples, the clouds swirled faster and faster. I was taken aback.

With mom at my side, I said, "Look at those clouds! Look how fast they're moving!"

"Do you see that?" I queried earnestly.

She didn't. She didn't see anything.

Oh, my God, I cocked my head to the side. *There!* In the sky between the towers, the clouds took on the shape of a slender lady holding a child! I burst into tears. I was scared and only glanced occasionally at her. I was frightened and humbled to gaze at her magnificence. I was awestruck.

"There! Between the steeples," I cried. "There are angels at her feet," I told mom.

Mom didn't see anything. I don't know how much time passed before the clouds faded away, and the vision ended. That image was forever burned into my mind. Looking at her in the clouds was like looking at a photo negative, shades of gray. However, mom said that there were no clouds in the sky.

When the image finally faded, I pleaded half to mom and half to myself, "Don't tell anyone! Don't tell anyone!"

Visibly upset and still sobbing, I lit up a cigarette. After all that time, I was still hooked on tobacco. Then, I heard the groans of the crowd of people around me. *It's because I'm smoking.* I was always conscious of other people and, more importantly, their reaction to me. I beat myself up for my actions more than anyone else could. I would come to understand why.

"I have to go to confession!" I ran off to the priests who were hearing confessions along the side of the building.

I chose the one with the handprinted sign: "English." I remember him fondly. He was an elderly Irish gentleman.

"Now, now," he said to calm me as tears washed down my cheeks. "The Blessed Mother is appearing to the children at this very moment."

"I know," I replied between sobs. "I saw her."

I will never forget his face. He looked right into my eyes as if he wanted to "see" as well.

"Bless me, Father, for I have sinned. My last confession was about ten years ago. I try to be good. But I'm afraid of people."

At the end of my confession, I recited the Act of Contrition, as was common practice.

"I will pray for you," the priest promised.

He was quite old thirty years ago. He probably has since passed away and is buried in a churchyard in Ireland. I believe he did pray for me, and, now, I pray for him.

I laid in bed that night and looked through the lace curtains into the starlit sky. Tears streamed out of my eyes. I tried not to make a sound as mom was sleeping in the next bunk. I felt so loved that night. I don't think I ever felt loved like that before. I will never forget. That was the highlight of my pilgrimage to the village of Medjugorje.

There are poles, good and evil, happy and sad. The visitation of the Blessed Mother was good, but I did have a rather unpleasant experience during my visit to the "old country." What was important to me was the beautiful memory of the spiritual happening that October evening. A memory I would retell in vivid detail to Dr. Andrews in a hypnotic trance the following month.

CHAPTER 12

The Mother of God

November 5, 1988

Back from Europe on October 17, 1988, I eagerly awaited my next appointment with my doctor. I always scheduled meetings for Saturday mornings, lest A Corp discovered that I was seeing a psychiatrist. Alas, the ever so special day finally arrived, and I carried a little wooden cross, wood-beaded rosary, and a booklet describing Medjugorje to present to Dr. Andrews. After cordial pleasantries, I anxiously described the fantastic happening in front of St. James Church.

It felt like an eternity waiting for him to invite me to the familiar black recliner. I eagerly concentrated on Dr. Andrew's soothing voice as he talked me into a deep meditative state. I usually began my tale by noticing my senses, describing a color or feeling. Today was different. The hypnotic story began quite suddenly when brilliant white light engulfed my "sight."

I jerked forward in my chair, immersed in a hypnotic trance. Instinctively, I knew this "light" was someone. It was like talking to a person right in front of me. But this spirit was a light I was somehow within.

"Who are you? I must know!" I begged out loud, "Who are you?" I needed to know with my entire being.

"I am the Mother of God," she stated.

I wept. I was so scared. I could not look directly at her because I felt awestruck, humbled, and unworthy.

"Don't be afraid," she soothingly said in my mind.

It was as if she were patting my hair down like you would do to calm a child.

"Am I doing wrong?" I cringed, asking.

"No," she replied to my surprise.

"I don't always want to be afraid of the fire," I said half in a question, half in prayer to her.

"You won't be," she stated emphatically in reassurance.

In past hypnosis sessions with Dr. Andrews, I acted out the part of a young woman named Marie Antoinette Chambre. Marie was a nurse to soldiers in another time and place, which I designated as 1868, France. This young lady was burned to death by an angry mob. That was why I was afraid of the fire.

The Mother of God, as she called herself, told me things in this trance. More than I can remember or maybe more than I should consciously know. However, I do remember as she faded away, I inquired, "Are you leaving me?"

"I will always be with you," she responded.

The vision and the light were gone.

"Don't tell anyone! Don't tell anyone!" I cried to Mom, who was at my side in the trance. "I have to go to confession!"

But now I know why I rushed off to the confessionals. I needed to get away from the people who showed displeasure at my cigarette. I needed to get away from them!

Then, "Bless me, Father," I said as my head dropped to my shoulder to signal that the hypnotic trance was over.

Thankfully, the hypnotic vision gave me much to think about at work—something on which to base hope. It kept me going.

Unfortunately, during the next week, I received terrible news by way of a letter. Dr. Andrews announced his retirement at the end of December 1988. I was devastated by the news. He had been my lifeline to sanity for the past three years. *What was I going to do without him?* I was angry and felt betrayed that he would leave me because I had grown close to him, and he was a father figure to me. I should have been happy for him. I had one more appointment in December, and I intended to show my appreciation to my friend and doctor.

CHAPTER 13

This Was God!

December 1988

This, my last visit with Dr. Andrews, was bitter-sweet. I arrived at the office with a little parcel of sweet treats for his retirement gift. We talked for forty minutes. He was leaving his practice to volunteer at the local veterans center. Finally, the time came for my last hypnotic trance with him.

This time I came up outside of my body. I was "flying" over mountains. It was incredible.

"I saw these mountains before," I began to relay my experience to Dr. Andrews.

I passed through a grand opening in the dark clouds where, like a winter sky, a silver-white light had shown through. The "other side," to my surprise, was like the night sky.

I told the doctor in amazement, "Lights are bursting like fireworks!"

It was a jubilant display of colors, an incredible sight to behold! I didn't have that horrible fear that always plagued me, even when I went to see this kindly gentleman, my own doctor.

"Is it a festival?" Dr. Andrews queried.

"No," I replied. "They're greeting me!" I said of the spiritual beings who were bursting into the colors of light.

The "lights" took me forward.

"I don't have to ask who this is!" I reported utterly in awe.

I was so humbled. I knew this was God!

"He's showing me a movie," I described. "But the time isn't right," I stated puzzled.

I watched intently, and it was like when I took the train to Philadelphia, the trees outside a blur through the windows of the speeding train. That is what I meant when I said the time isn't right. It was as if time sped up!

I remained quiet in the black recliner beside the doctor's desk for quite some time.

Dr. Andrews probed, "Are you still watching it?"

"Yes."

Finally, I announced, "It's done."

I felt as if God bestowed on me a great honor. In utter humility and genuine bewilderment at the tribute He paid to me, I asked, "Why me?"

"He's raising me up!" I exclaimed.

It was as if I was in the palms of His hands, but He was light! He raised me above Him to honor me!

"There are stars above Him.".

But alas, I was coming "home." Or was I leaving my real "home?" Anyway, the trance had ended.

My head sank to my shoulder. The fantastic story was over.

I believe that God showed me my life that day. As I left his office, Dr. Andrews gave me a hearty hug.

"Thank you for everything!" I solemnly offered.

This doctor doesn't know it, but at least for a short while, he preserved my sanity.

CHAPTER 14

The Hope for Relief

1989

I struggled in my dysfunctional office environment for years. I tried to help myself after the ill-fated joke in 1986. We did not have a union to go to for help at A Corp. The only thing I could do was move out of the accounting department. In November 1986, I went to personnel and put my name on the supposed transfer list. I soon learned that was not the way it was done there. You had to know someone to get a transfer. It was apparent when I saw coworkers, who had not gone through the personnel department, change jobs. For years I was stuck on the bogus list without so much as an interview. I believed that I couldn't leave the company because I was there for seventeen years, making a good deal of money without a college degree. I supported Bill and me. He apprenticed with a sign painter for years and was quite good. But he didn't have a job; no income. Determined to get away from the trio, I got the names of the managers of the advertising and technical writing departments and sent them my resume along with samples of my writing.

To my delight, Mr. Billings, in advertising, responded with an invitation for a tour of his department. I worked up my courage and went into Steve with great trepidation.

"Steve," I hesitantly began, "I was invited by Mr. Billings, the manager of advertising, to tour his department. I want to go over there."

"You know Julija; you can go. But if he offers you a job, Elwood and I can stop you from taking it. You didn't go through personnel."

My heart sank to my feet. They didn't like me. *Why would they stop me from leaving? Why?*

I was so upset that evening. Steve's words went round and round in my head. He wasn't going to let me leave. I had to get away from them, and he wasn't going to let me leave. I tossed and turned in bed, crunching up into the fetal position. This was so important to me. *How could they do this to me?*

Even with Steve's threat, I set an appointment, and the day of my advertising tour finally arrived. I wore a dark tan tailored skirt and jacket. I certainly looked professional! What a disappointment the whole situation turned out to be. Mr. Billings was not my guide. It was an underling, a supervisor named Mr. Vance.

"How do you know Mr. Billings?" he bluntly asked me.

When I replied that I did not know him personally, he turned cold. I knew what his agenda was, and I did not fit in there. I would have moved from the pot into the fire as they say.

Shortly after that, one of the accounting analysts left our office, and his job was open. It was an office at the other end of our department. I desperately needed to get away from the venomous trio. Also, it would have been a grade up the promotion scale for me. I had hoped for relief!

I wasted no time when I heard of the vacancy. "Steve, I would like to be considered for Dan's job."

Now I certainly was well qualified with my accounting experience, and I had the company seniority. I needed that job.

But I saw the writing on the wall when Steve responded, "You just want to move away from where you sit!"

I did. I needed to move away from them.

The next thing I knew, my close friend, Linda, was seated in Steve's office with Elwood also present with the door closed. A searing heat drenched my mind. I was utterly crushed. Yes, they offered Linda, who had much less experience and seniority then I had, Dan's position. She accepted. I was steeped in depression and hopelessly sunk into myself.

CHAPTER 15

Get Out the Straitjacket!

1989

The situation deteriorated. Sheila followed me wherever I went in the office. When I talked to Michelle, my coworker, Sheila, would walk by my desk. What they were doing to me was so evident that my coworker and I would wait for her to come. If it wasn't Sheila, it was Steve or Elwood. She especially followed me when I went to the bathroom. I was thin, and I believe she thought she would catch me throwing up like she did. She was anorexic and bulimic, so skinny that her huge brown eyes stood out almost alien-like.

Once I went into the ladies' room and waited for her to come in. "I was waiting for you. I knew you would follow me."

"You're paranoid," she responded.

Elwood always waited in the bathroom hallway to see the upset look on my face when I came out of the restroom. Once, I slipped into the bathroom through the back of the office. Sheila's friend saw me, and sure enough, here came Sheila. Her friend couldn't even look at me when I went out of the restroom. She was guilty.

43

I began to use the bathroom downstairs. One day I was downstairs, and I saw Steve in the hallway reading the bulletin board. *He never did that! Was he down there to follow me too?*

Seated back at my desk, I saw Steve return. But instead of going into his office, he went right into Elwood's office and closed the door! *Was he reporting me to Elwood?*

God! What could I do? By then, I was trapped in a state of severe depression. I turned inward. I had been seeing a new Psychiatrist, Dr. Ambrose, and talking to him helped. But it was not like the release of anxiety I experienced when I used hypnosis with Dr. Andrews. Dr. Ambrose wanted me to take medication to calm me, but I refused. I heard it made you gain weight. I regret that choice.

Every day going to my job was like torture. The trio devised phony surveys and noise memos, which said we can't talk at our desk, all to trip me up. It sounds paranoid, but I still had my wits about me, and I researched their attempted surveys. Also, a credit manager who was my friend told me the memo was directed at me. I kept the proof after all these years. I couldn't destroy it.

One day, I was downstairs to go to the vending machine area and passed the lunchroom. Sheila was sitting at one of the tables. I was petrified and went about my business downstairs, quite upset at seeing her, and headed back to the second floor.

Sheila sauntered by my desk and immediately went into Elwood's office. She thought I followed her to the lunchroom! She was elated that she finally got a reaction from me. I would not ever do anything to retaliate against them. I never gave them ammunition to discipline me or to think they were getting to me.

Elwood was elated, as well! He wasted no time running into Steve's office.

I heard. "Get out the straitjacket. She's gonna go!" Elwood announced with that evil smile on his face.

Steve replied, "It's probably for the best."

Tell me, how could it have been for the best? That day Steve may as well have stuck a dagger through my heart, and worse, my family as well. They may as well have said, "Crucify her!"

CHAPTER 16

There Must Be Peace!

January 1987

I previously mentioned a young French nurse named Marie Antoinette Chambre. This is an odd place to begin her story, but I believe that endings are the start of new beginnings. And so, it was for Marie. This was to be the first session that I recalled the maiden while under hypnosis with Dr. Andrews back in 1987

Once again in the comfortable recliner:

"And when you are ready, just allow whatever will help you with where you are today to come up," he instructed.

"I can't see." My eyes squinted into slits. My sight was painful, as if I came into the sunlight from a very dark place.

"The light hurts my eyes," I told my doctor as I strained to see.

"Water. I need water?" My parched tongue was sticking to the roof of my mouth.

I could barely speak. I felt this sensation in my trance. At one point, I asked Dr. Andrews if I was talking funny. I don't know if the people in my trance who were leading me through the crowd that gathered around me gave me water or not, I don't believe they did.

My eyes were adjusting. I saw a narrow cobblestone street with tall buildings, and a wooden sign was hanging on a bracket above a door on one of the buildings. My hands shook. I was aware of my wedding band pinging against Dr. Andrews' wooden desk or the recliner.

"Don't do this!" I begged the angry mob who surrounded me.

"You are hungry. Don't do this." I pled.

I pleaded to these people for my life. I don't remember what I said.

"The women have coverings over their heads." I described it to Dr. Andrews.

I sensed I was being led through the crowd. My hands bound in front of me. Shaking with fear, I looked up at the sky. Then I saw it! The sun, a ball of brilliant orange shown above the roof lines.

Suddenly, from my head to my feet, all the fear drained from me. I have never been without fear in my life until that moment. There was such joy!

"I'm not afraid!" I laughed and cried with joy. "I'm not afraid!"

There was a lady off in the distance behind the crowd.

"Who is that lady in pink?" I wondered. "She's smiling. She knows I'm not afraid." I can still see the beautiful smiling face of the woman dressed head to toe in pink. I felt loved by her like she knew me.

But then a man dressed in black with a black top hat yanked my hands up and bound me to a metal post. I still remember how I acted it out for Dr. Andrews in that chair.

"He started my dress on fire," I told the doctor.

The shouts of the people faded, getting more distant, as I felt myself twirling through the stars. It was as if I was tumbling up and up through the stars far away from the mob.

"Peace. There is peace here." I stated.

I didn't feel as if I was missing my body. But I had to be a spirit or energy. I was still myself—whole. I came upon two bright lights. I instinctively knew they were someone. They were beings.

"Who are you?" I questioned.

"Messengers," they responded. "You must go back!"

"No. I can't go back. I'm too weak."

"You won't be. People will help you."

I was saddened and distressed.

They spoke again. "She said there must be peace, and they won't listen to her. You must go back and save people- like Mr. Barton."

With my Catholic religious background, I believed the "she" who they spoke of was the Blessed Mother.

Mr. Barton was a politician who killed himself on television in the 1980s. I felt terrible about it. It was, to me, one of those happenings where you remember what you were doing when you heard something terrible had happened. I did not know what this meant at the time of the hypnosis. But I may know what Mr. Barton was feeling. I have felt the same thing and have come to understand the feelings of helplessness.

Then Dr. Andrews asked me, "Does Sheila remind you of someone from your past?"

I nodded, "The man who started my dress on fire."

And that was the end of the hypnosis session with Dr. Andrews where I met my death, and perhaps, life after death. Unfortunately, the fearlessness did not remain when I came out of the trance.

CHAPTER 17

The Psychosis

January 18, 1990

If I had to name the day when my mind flipped into psychosis, it was this one. My husband, Bill, left for an ice fishing trip with my cousins the day before.

"Please, don't go!" I begged him. "I'll dress up in my corset and stockings," I tried to bargain with him to stay.

He went anyway, and I was left by myself. *I know it's going to be bad!* He always drank too much. He's going to cause some problems. Last Sunday, I called every bar he frequented looking for him.

"Is Bill there?" I asked.

"Haven't seen him?" the annoyed barmaid replied.

I drove all through Milltown, searching for him. I could not find his Ford pickup anywhere. It wasn't the first time that he "disappeared."

Where does he go?

It was Thursday, and I had another bad day at work the day before. The systems analyst was teaching me how to type my month-end reconciliation on Excel. It was a disaster. A part of me wouldn't acknowledge the shaking hand phobia. Sitting at that computer with the analyst watching me was one of those days. When my hands began to tremble, I saw that familiar stunned look on his face. I'd seen it many times before.

Why didn't I tell him that my hands shake when someone watches me instead of acting like everything was okay? Bill was in denial with the alcohol. Somewhere in my mind, I was "protecting" myself from the truth as well.

Thankfully I had taken a vacation day from work, and, surrounded by computer books on the sofa, my thoughts turned to Bill's suspicious behavior. And that was the moment that I, Julija Rudolf, snapped into psychosis.

Where does he go? What is he hiding? I began to pull the porn magazines out from under the bedroom vanity. They were not soft porn, either. Bondage! Swingers! *God, what is he into?*

Then, under the steps, there were video cassettes. Everywhere! There was porn everywhere! I found a tape made of a male stripper at one of his clubs. *Was he gay?*

And then in my now broken mind, I found it. There was a white tissue under the bed!

How did that get there? I tried to see if it was from our tissue box on the bathroom vanity. Ah-ha! It was not the same! It's not from here! I was crazed! *I'm struggling at work to keep us afloat, and what is he doing at home during the day?* Now I was sure. *He was cheating on me. He was making a fool out of me!*

I was mentally gone by the time Sunday rolled around, and Bill returned home from the trip.

"I found it, Bill! I know what you're doing! I have the evidence." I confronted him.

He had no idea what I was talking about! I didn't even tell him what I thought he did! I would not tell him I based his so-called crime on a tissue I found under the bed. A tissue. Oh, he was an alcoholic for sure, and undoubtedly "guilty" of addiction to pornography. I was no longer a rational person. I was sure he was bringing women to the house, but what I did not know is that I flipped into psychosis that day. I completely exited reality! In hindsight, I can only imagine the stress I placed on Bill.

CHAPTER 18

The Broken Mind

Things were indeed tense at home. Bill drank so much last night at the club, and he crawled in the door. He couldn't walk. Even though I didn't sleep at all that night, I was wide awake for work on Monday morning. It was different today.

I was anxious to get to work. I didn't feel safe with Bill. In my mind, he had become my enemy. He was using me. I was sure of it. Once at my desk, I found it hard to sit still. I was usually so withdrawn. Not today. It was my fourth trip in an hour to the hallway water fountain when I noticed Elwood standing outside his office watching me. The water smelled foul, but it didn't stop me from imbibing it. God, it smelled of diesel fuel. I had to keep drinking it, though. With Elwood there, I watched myself as if looking through a mirror. I had to maintain a stoic face. I couldn't let him see my distress, and I couldn't admit it to myself, either. But that was the way my day went. That was the way the last four years went.

I began to throw up at home, especially when Bill was there. But I kept drinking water. More and more. *Was Bill poisoning me?* I believed that I had to wash the poison out of my system.

Bill began to act as strangely as me. Erotic sex came to the forefront of our lives. I was drinking more water, while Bill drank more and more beer. One morning there was a red Ford Taurus parked in front of our house. Psychosis feeds on itself. Everything means something. In my sick mind, they were a part of my imaginary plot. *Who were they?* I watched every move Bill made. Everything. I searched for his truck when he was not home. I kept track of his mileage. *Where was he going?* Little did I know the horrendous stress I was putting on my husband. Back to the car parked in front of our house. There was no reason for it to be there. *Who was it?* I had an in. Bill's brother, Joe, was Township Commissioner.

I explained to Joe about Bill acting strangely. I told him that I believed he was cheating on me. I told him that Bill was into something terrible. Maybe even illegal. But it wasn't his fault because someone was giving him mind-control drugs. Bill wasn't himself. Joe, being the good brother that he was, agreed to run the license plate for me.

Soon, Joe called to tell me that the car parked in front of our house for days was registered to a pharmaceutical company. It was a drug salesman. It couldn't be any worse. Bill WAS poisoning me. That's why I kept getting sick. That's why I needed to drink all the water. I needed to flush the poison out of my system. *Bill! Oh, Bill, what was I going to do?*

I reasoned with him, but Bill was acting stranger and stranger. He was as fragile as me. He would come home at night talking to himself. I didn't know there was such a thing as alcoholic schizophrenia or that I was in a Bipolar psychosis.

One night it got to be too much. "Just because I have murder on tape," he said tauntingly.

It wasn't him! He looked so evil like he was another person.

"Did you ever have an abortion?"

What was he talking about?

And then, "You better watch you don't kill yourself. How much insurance do you have anyway?" he quizzed me with wild eyes.

He wanted me to kill myself! It was all I could take. I was afraid for my life and left him that night. I went to live with my mom, who was scared for me. I did not tell her Bill was poisoning me, but I did tell Dr. Ambrose.

I told the young Dr. Ambrose about the pharmaceutical salesman. I told him Bill was poisoning me, and he wasn't doing it of his inclination. Someone was giving him mind-control drugs.

One night at mom's, I finally drank too much water. I was so sick. I felt like I could go into a coma. The only thing that kept me awake was my one-year-old nephew sitting on mom's lap, twirling a sock by a string. Mom was telling me stories of World War II and all the soldiers who came to Milltown. Those two saved my life that night. I thought for sure I was going to die. I don't know what possessed me to, but I called Bill at the club.

He came to the phone. "I just want to tell you," I said, "if you're trying to kill me, you succeeded."

Bill was distraught and told me, "I'll be right there."

It didn't take him long to get to mom's house. I was sitting in the basement. That was where I spent most of my time. I couldn't smoke upstairs, and I was inhaling one after the other. I was crying.

"Did you ever drink so much water that it came out of your nose?" I questioned Bill in rebuke. "Did you ever have diarrhea so bad that only water came out?"

Bill was extremely upset. "You don't deserve this." He said solemnly. "I'm taking you to the hospital," he stated.

I was dying. I knew my kidneys shut down, and so I agreed.

On the way to the hospital, "I need salt. I need salt." I cried out in despair, trying to hold onto life.

Then I heard the Mother of God say, "Before the night is over, you will talk to Dr. Bruce."

Dr. Bruce was my family doctor. I was going to the hospital late at night, and it didn't make sense that I would talk to Dr. Bruce.

I didn't have to wait for an emergency room bed. They took me right away and hooked me up to an IV. I was convinced something suspicious was happening. Things weren't normal, and these people were in on it.

The doctor came in shortly after the nurse drew blood. She had a syringe that she was going to insert into my IV.

"What is that?" I demanded.

"It's only potassium. You need potassium." She replied. "You need to give us a urine specimen."

I knew they were in on it. *I can't do that! My God, they'll find out Bill was poisoning me.* I refused. I had to protect him.

Finally, I needed to use the bathroom. I felt my kidneys working again. I was better, and I had to get out of here. I ripped the intravenous needle from my hand. Blood squirted out all over. I took the cotton ball that was placed on the inside of my elbow, where they took blood and put it over the wound. I got dressed.

"I'm checking out," I told the nurse at the counter in the emergency room. The doctor ran over.

"If this happens to you again, you could die." She pleaded for me to stay.

"I'm better now," I responded flatly.

The doctor had the receptionist contact, Dr. Bruce. The next thing I knew, I was talking to my family doctor on the telephone. The prophecy had come to pass.

"Should I stay?" I trusted Dr. Bruce.

"Yes. If you have what they say, you need to stay."

Bill sat with me all night. He held my hand tightly and convinced me that it was okay to give a urine sample. As it turned out, I had a bladder and kidney infection. It was probably from the foul water that I was drinking at work. Of course, in my paranoia, I still believed Bill was poisoning me. Yes, it was poison absorbed through your skin. It was everywhere. I always thought the drug salesman was giving him mind-control drugs.

I was in the hospital for two days while they gave me IV antibiotics. When finally released, my sister came to take me back to mom's house.

Bill brought me beautiful flowers during my hospital stay. However, I would not touch or take the flower arrangements home because I believed they were poisoned too. But the most beautiful thing happened. My sister picked up the flowers for me and dumped them in the trash can. She believed Bill was poisoning me too. But she was willing to give up her life for me. And that is love.

I will never forget walking into mom's that day. *Well, I guess if the world is going to end and the story of Revelation in the bible is real, it might just as well be happening now!*

That's the way it continued in my broken mind for the next year and a half.

CHAPTER 19

Leave!

1990

I liked staying with mom. For the first time in a long while, I felt safe. But Bill called me all the time.

"Please come home," he cried, "I need you."

I even began to trust him again. I told Dr. Ambrose that I wasn't being poisoned any longer. Bill and I began to go out on dates. It was quite romantic. But I was always aware of the people following me. There were good guys, and there were evil people. I was still deep in psychosis.

One spring day, I stopped at Bill's to get some clothes. He wasn't home, but the house was trashed. A lamp was on the floor with a bent-up lampshade, and the antique oak table in the kitchen was thrown over. *Oh God, it was one of his rages. It's because of me.* In my sickness, I had to fix this as I fixed everything. And a week or so before Easter 1990, I moved back in with Bill.

Everything was normal, except my glasses were bugged by the police, and there was a receiver planted in my recent dental work. I went to work as though nothing was odd, though. I had one foot in reality and one foot in a dream world. I took care of household chores, like paying bills. However, I was making the bills as fast as I was paying them. I was shopping all the time; jewelry, clothes, anything that caught my eye. Money meant nothing in the world that I was in.

It was evident that I had lost my mind. Elwood and Steve did this to me, and they knew it. They tried to fix it. Steve and I had moved to the other end of the office away from Sheila and Elwood. Paul told me it was because they thought I would get better there. I don't believe that Paul realized the seriousness of my mental state. Steve told me not to mention anything to Paul. He said that he tells Sheila everything. Even in my sickness, I knew that was not true. Paul knew what Sheila was like. Steve and Elwood were afraid of what I could tell Paul about them, or maybe they were trying to coverup the extent of how much they harmed me.

I made it through the summer. However, the change of seasons and the changes at work affected my mania. I was deteriorating. I stopped going into Steve's office because I believed they were trying to set me up with cameras. I wouldn't even deliver his mail. They were trying to trap me somehow. What I didn't realize was that they wanted me out of there. Due to my illness, they needed me to leave. That would fix it all for them.

One day, they locked me out of my computer. *How could I possibly do my work?* I heard the voice for the first time. "Leave!" he said. This voice did not like what they were doing to me. Things were not right or reasonable. So, that day I went home.

I didn't believe that work was real anymore. I did not go to work the next day, either. What's worse, I didn't call in that I was going to be off, a major no-no at A Corp. But it didn't matter, it was just a game.

The day after my unauthorized leave, I went back to work. I got my morning coffee as if nothing happened. Elwood and Steve were waiting for me, and I was called before them into Steve's office.

"You were off yesterday and did not call in. Why?" Elwood demanded.

I'd had enough. I could not contain my anger anymore.

"Maybe I was doing this to you!" And I proceeded to give him the middle finger.

Elwood got the biggest smile on his face because he had me. I finally warranted discipline. It didn't matter that both a credit manager and Steve displayed their anger that way all the time. But it was me. And they were trying to get rid of me. Well, I had my say that day.

"Elwood," I said, "You were depressed since your divorce. You will never be happy."

Then came Steve's turn with my wrath.

"And Steve," I prophesied, "You do have trouble at home."

I finally spoke up after four years of silence.

They sent me home that day in December, and I never went back. Dr. Ambrose talked me into applying for disability, and that was it for my employment at A Corp. For the longest time, I got dressed in the morning as if I was going to work. I worked there for seventeen years, and it had become my identity. At least I had time to make Christmas cookies, and all the foods mom taught me how to make.

CHAPTER 20

The Book of Revelation

1991

I no longer had office intrigues to occupy my crippled mind. I was pulled in another direction. I developed an intense fascination with the last book of the Bible's New Testament, The Book of Revelation.

Some say Revelation is a cipher for political events in ancient history. But most people will say it tells of a forthcoming apocalypse or end of times. In my psychosis, the end *was* happening.

I had a significant role in this play. But was I the Lamb, or was I the Bride? *Oh God, all these people following me. Do they think I'm the Anti-Christ? No! No! Stay away from me! I'm not a public person.* And so, the neurosis went round and round. It became my new game. I was drawn to Revelations 6: 1-4:

Revelation 6 WEB

1 I saw that the Lamb opened one of the seven seals, and I heard one of the four living creatures saying, as with a voice of thunder, "Come and see!" 2 And behold, a white horse, and he who sat on it had a bow. A crown was given to him, and he came out conquering, and to conquer. 3 When he opened the second seal, I heard the second living creature saying,

> *"Come!" 4 Another came out: a red horse. To him who sat on it was given the power to take peace from the earth, and that they should kill one another. There was given to him a great sword.*

This verse mirrored a hypnosis session I had with Dr. Andrews back in 1987. It was another segment in the life of the French nurse, Marie Antoinette Chambre. Again, I wondered, was I her in a past life? I was sure this trance was prophesied in the Book of "Revealing."

In that familiar chair, Dr. Andrews talked me into my usual dream-like state. I began rapid eye movement, signaling that I was now "under." The tale unfolded with a quickness. Suddenly, I became animated. In the first "light" of trance, I sat on the ground and stared at two rows of large brass buttons down the front of a royal blue uniform jacket. I instinctively knew it was a soldier.

"He's in my lap," I reported as his head fell into the folds of my dress.

When I spoke, I tasted and felt gritty dirt in my mouth from dust horse hooves were kicking up into the air.

"He's dying. I can see it in his eyes," I sobbed. "He knows he's dying." Tears streamed down my cheeks even as my eyes were closed in my trance.

"My tears are mixing with his blood," I blurted out to the doctor.

The full red cuff of his sleeve reached up to my face.

"He wiped a tear from my cheek," I told Dr. Andrews.

"You must be an angel," the dying man whispered as he took his last breath.

"He died!" I cried in sheer grief. "He died!" I was inconsolable.

I sat in that recliner and wept for some time.

"They're still fighting!" I screamed in disgust through the din of the battle going on around me.

"A man just died, and they're still fighting!" Anger welled up inside of me.

My eyes were drawn to a white horse that reared up amid the battle.

"The rider is dressed in red." I hesitantly described it to the doctor.

He swung a long thick sword in the air.

"He's wearing a red helmet with something sticking up on top of it," I reported. By this time, I saw his face and looked into his dark eyes.

I was livid. "They're still fighting! A man died, and they're still fighting!"

Finally, I sensed the story ending, and my head dropped to my shoulder. I came out of the hypnosis quite drained. It was over.

I will never forget this episode in the life of Marie Antoinette. I still can see the "rider's" face. *What did it all mean? Why did I "see" this?*

CHAPTER 21

The Psychotic World

1991

It was another endless day of psychosis. I played my music loud; Peter Gabriel, Genesis, and Bob Dylan echoed throughout our little A-frame home. Bill was downstairs in the garage, working on something. He would have never tolerated my music selection.

That day, I was on the down-cycle of my mania.

Without warning, I was thrown into the bowels of hell. "I can't breathe!" I cried out. "I can't breathe!" as I gasped for air.

Was I dying? I felt a tremendous weight placed on me. I stood there and leaned into the "arms" holding me up as if I fell into the gusting wind.

"I know who you are!" I emphatically stated.

The voice in my head made me believe he was God, but I knew the truth, he was the demon. In my delusions, I thought that I stole secrets from the "dark side" of the wheel of life as I cycled up and down. I stole secrets that would save humankind. I could know all the wonders of the universe, and I had answers to the unanswered mysteries that scientists searched for. I was becoming a physicist, a doctor. The demon thought he had me fooled to do his bidding, to rob my soul, but God chose me. I was strong. *I am the Ark of the Covenant.*

Well, that was a typical day in my psychotic world in 1990 and 1991. At least until July 28, 1991. I open my original journal entries, although disjointed, to you:

July 15, 1991

Half of the time, I feel like I am in a trance. I do the weirdest things, and I can see myself doing them, and I feel like I am a computer program or something. I say things, and it's like it's not me talking. And then when I think about what I said, it sounds like I said something else. I don't know. I believe that I have gone around the bend.

I feel like the dog when he's looking at something, but we (humans) can't see anything there. I think I am looking at something, but I can't see it with my human eyes. I believe I am looking at something with some inner eye.

A THIRD EYE

I am either psychotic, or I have some ESP.

And that's not all. I hear things (people) "lights" are talking to me all the time. And I hear them the same way that I see. It's like having a third ear or something. I don't know! I think this whole thing is big trouble!

When this whole thing started, there was a time that I thought a bunch of "Bible-bangers" was after me. Boy, was I ever pissed off! I said to myself, "If these people who are giving me such a hard time are doing it because of their religious fanaticism, I was going to get them good." Little do I know how much trouble I could be in. Mucho problema! (These "lights" could be you know what's!)

This could be bigger than I think! How am I going to get out of this one? I might be doomed!

And then there is that voice I can hear loud and clear! He told me that he was a priest! I gave him such a hard time!

Now that I think about this, I tried to be nice to him at first, and he wasn't responsive to my sweet talk. Your mom told me in so many words that you weren't used to warm people!

July 16, 1991

It was cold. My car stalled partway up the driveway. I let it drift back down to the bottom. You told me not to put on the brakes, and I didn't. My car ran into the back of Bill's truck. I told you that I trusted you so much that I did exactly what you wanted me to, and you let me hit my husband's truck. You told me not to get out of my car until you told me to, and I listened to you again (even though I just hit the truck because you told me not to brake). We are somehow bonded, and I trust you with my life. I have seen you defend me (even though I am not sure how or what was happening). I just knew somehow you were doing that. All these people buzzing around me made me feel like they were trying to tell me that you were evil. Sometimes it made me wonder if that might be true.

July 16, 1991

You told me that you were a priest. But I believe that you are for all peoples. I believe that you are universal, or at least you should be. Am I wrong?

July 17, 1991

When the psychosis things started, the voice asked my permission to "move" me. I asked if it would benefit people. The voice said that it would. So, I said, "okay."

July 18, 1991

The voice told me that even when I don't hear or feel him moving my limbs, he is still with me.

July 20, 1991

Compulsive disorders are tricks we used to hide secrets from ourselves.

Phobias are the same brand of trick.

Uncover the secret, and the habit/phobia will "extinguish itself."

July 21, 1991

Uncle Ray once told me that my dad would be proud of me. Somehow, I know that he is proud of me.

July 22, 1991

I don't understand why time feels so strange to me. It feels like spirals. Like a funnel. Like it's meeting or joining.

Only with God can you achieve nirvana. Man cannot achieve it on his own.

My family and friends were my most prized possession, and for some reason, they are beyond my reach right now.

I never realized that my constant search for inner peace was a search for God himself. A search for Nirvana. If I would have known that, I think it might have been easier traveling because he was there all the time. In other words, I thought I had only my strength to pull from to see him. But if he didn't want me to see him, I wouldn't have. I kept trying and trying and wouldn't quit, even though it sometimes scared me. He must have pitied me. (Because I am his child).

I had a whole army of angels and saints with me! What a vision! There are no words that could describe the beauty! The most important ones were the most beautiful! Those who sit closest to God!

July 25, 1991

It seems that people have managed to reduce me to nothing but a lump of flesh. I don't even know why. I wonder what I have done to deserve the treatment I receive.

CHAPTER 22

A Harsh Reality

July 28, 1991

Today is a fantastic day for me! God is taking me to my favorite bookstore at Union Square. What present is he going to pick out for me today? I was so excited that it felt like my old TR6 drove itself there!

I could smell all the wonderful books that lined the shelves! But that day was different. God was picking out a goodbye present for me. Somehow, I knew the story, the psychosis was ending. Time wound down. He told me a couple of days before that it would end in a "V." I knew that he meant the funnel of time I was caught up in was closing.

It didn't take me long to pick out something. God chose for my gift the *Tao Te Ching* (an ancient Chinese text that tells the "way of life"). I held it tight against my chest. I had no idea what lay ahead of me. But I would find out in a couple of hours.

Just as I snapped into psychosis, I snapped out of it suddenly that summer afternoon. I was severely manic from January 18, 1990, to July 28, 1991. To understand the pain that I suffered coming out of a year and a half of psychosis, here are my journal entries from 1991. The first one is when I realized I lost touch with reality and, consequently, lost my job.

Julija Rudolf

July 28, 1991

I just finished reading what I wrote in this journal. I can't believe that I went through a situation like that with my mind. I think I was really "out of it." I feel sane (I hope) once again. What was that? When I was going through it, I felt like I was "out of this world." I felt like I was talking to and responding to spirits. It must truly have been a real psychosis. I remember feeling it wind down—like I knew it was going to end. I hope it did. I must get back to the "real" world and figure out how to pull my life back together. I wouldn't wish what I went through since January 1990, on anyone. It was like extremes, like moving from extreme anguish to extreme euphoria. I must get my life back together, somehow. I don't know where even to start. I don't know why this happened to me in the first place.

August 8, 1991

Nothing like waking up from illness to discover that you don't have a job. After seventeen years of working at a prominent electronic corporation and making twenty-five grand a year, I am out in the cold.

My main effort right now should be to get well. I feel rather rotten right now, physically and mentally. My main advantage is that I don't have the psychosis anymore. Just like I snapped into it, I snapped out of it.

It's hard to think of some of the things that I did and thought. I know that I hallucinated during the psychosis. I'm beginning to think that I heard things as well.

What are we going to do for money? I'm the breadwinner. Bill, my husband, is a starving artist. In other words, he doesn't make a living. How am I going to get another job?

I guess if I must, I can try to get a job in a department store or fast food restaurant if they would even hire me. I think that my chances of getting a regular office job would be better if I went to college for two years.

September 5, 1991

Let go and let God. That's an Al-Anon saying, and I have been telling myself that a lot. Yes, I am going to Al-Anon now. I just had to go somewhere for help—for companionship. You see, Bill is always at the neighborhood bar. He is an alcoholic in denial, and it played a significant part in my mental illness. Well anyway, I'm not in the deep dark dumps that I was in before. I feel a little bit better since the antidepressants. I feel more normal, and I can't believe the situation I am in. How in the hell do I manage to get into such predicaments? I truly don't know. But if I can survive this one, it will be a small miracle.

September 6, 1991

Doctor appointment today. Not much is happening. I had to get expensive pills for $75. I feel hopeless today. There is not much of a future to look forward to. It looks bleak. There is simply no dignity in becoming mentally ill. I would rather have a disease that would eventually kill me instead of day after day of depression and worries about the future, which looks bleak anyway. It's kind of like hell on earth for me. I want it to end. That's all. Just end. Maybe with some dignity. I am so tired of this paralysis that cloaks me. I don't think anyone could understand unless they have been there. I don't think they could understand. It's too hard and too complicated. It's too painful, but it's a pain that you can't see. I don't believe you can imagine it either. If you break a bone, it's more understandable because there is something there that you can imagine. This mental thing is more painful than when I broke my leg in the eighth grade. But the pain is all over me now. It's painful to live and breathe. I can't explain it, and I wouldn't wish it on anyone. No one! It's hell. I'm in tears now. I feel sorry for myself. I just wanted to be a normal person. It doesn't seem like that is to be right now. The pain is too great. I don't know how much more of this I can take. I don't know. It's like there is a spell cast on me—an invisible weight holding me down. I wish I could put this into words better. I can't explain it so that someone would know or understand it. I would want someone to understand. I would want that because I didn't understand before it happened to me. I never understood it. Maybe I still don't understand completely. It's a lot to deal with.

I hate when I feel myself slipping away like this. I feel like I am on the verge of going crazy. Oh Lord, this won't do anymore. What am I going to do to keep sane?

When I was little and had teeth removed, I went to sleep with the ether mask on my face. I dreamt that the nurse was spinning round and round in the mask. Now, I feel that way. Like I am trapped in that mask and spinning round and round in the darkness. It's just a part of this illness. That's all it is—just a part of this illness.

Is there any way out of this? I can't see any. I can't see my way out of this. Maybe the future will be brighter. Maybe it will somehow change. I always felt bad for my uncle, who suffered shell shock from the war. Now I can see myself like he was. I feel like a real mental case right now. As someone, you would see on TV sitting in a chair and just staring into space. That's the way I feel.

You know, I can somehow understand how a person can be so desperate as to commit suicide. Pain in the body is bad. But mind pain affects the whole body. I hate to write this, but I have been obsessed with suicide almost ever since I came out of the psychosis. I don't want to spend the rest of my life as I am now. The rest of my life—how ironic. I feel like a vegetable. I feel like a real mental case, which I am now coming to believe.

I always felt like I had to take care of people. Like I have to keep things right for them. That's why this is such a horrible thing for me. Because I can't do anything for people anymore, I can't work now and bring in some income. I get insurance checks, but that's only good for two years. God, suppose things don't change, and I still feel like this basket case. Oh, God! The way I'm always bitching in this book makes me feel like I am selfish. But it's not only my pain that I can feel. I can feel Bill's pain, and I can feel pain in my family (pain for me). I can feel myself somehow withdrawing into myself. I don't want to even go anywhere anymore—not to the mall, not to the corner store, not anywhere at all. I once told my husband that I didn't think I was going to make it through this one. I don't know if he would remember me saying that. I feel myself distancing from the world. I didn't want to grocery shop today. I didn't want to leave home. I feel like I can end up like that woman I saw on a television program. She was in an institution, and she just sat there and stared. I could become like that woman. That's why I don't think that I am a well person.

I just took a walk around the block, and I feel mentally better somehow. I feel stimulated—maybe the antidepressants are going to kick in now. Dr. Ambrose said that it takes a while for them to work. If I felt this way all the time, I would have no problem working again. This is probably wishful thinking on my part. I am bored, though. I have to learn how to relax and enjoy myself a little bit—a teensy little bit. If only I could take advantage of this time that I am off. If I can manage to get another job, I might be working for the rest of my life. I should enjoy this break a little bit—just a little bit.

September 8, 1991

I want to be a normal person. I want to enjoy things like normal people do. I don't get into anything anymore. I need to make myself do things. When I started having trouble at work, I stopped doing things. I used to sew and make clothes using Vogue patterns. I made dolls dressed in Eastern European clothing for Bill's family. I even made drapes for our house, which Bill built in 1973 before we were married. You know, I should have quit my job and found something else. I only hurt myself by staying there. But I was frozen. I couldn't make any moves. I couldn't do anything. I was just frozen. I wonder if I can thaw out somehow. You know, I am still frozen. I still can't do anything. I wonder if I will ever be right again. Sometimes it doesn't feel like I will be. Most of the time, it feels like I will be this mental case forevermore. God, I want to be normal so bad.

Sometimes, lately, I can feel the psychosis in me. I can feel like another part of me or something. It's hard to explain.

I believe this mental illness was brewing in me for a long, long time now. Then suddenly, the shit hit the fan.

I wonder if it's my fault that I flipped out. Is it through my fault? I didn't even know how this happened. I had no idea I flipped out. I didn't know that

I did. I am still waiting for antidepressants to kick in. Dr. Ambrose says that it takes a while for them to start working. I want to be well. I want to get better.

Mental illness is an odd disease to have. It's like when I talk to people about it, they are afraid to talk about it or something. It's like they want to avoid talking about it. What a stigma the disease has.

I just took a walk around the block. I was hoping that I would get the same boost from it as I did yesterday. It didn't work yet.

September 10, 1991

I wonder if I am taking enough of a dose of the medications. It seems like I should be better than I am by now. Maybe I am not trying hard enough to get better. I did notice today, I feel more relaxed, and I can sit in one place for a while instead of jumping all over the place. That is a definite improvement. Muscles are not pulling as much today as they were yesterday.

Today, I thought to myself that maybe my life isn't over yet. That is good! It's been a long time since I felt good! And I'm smiling. But will it last?

CHAPTER 23

Finding Employment

December 1991

Five months after I snapped out of psychosis, I sat on a long wooden bench in the dingy old state building. I was an hour early as usual. I was waiting for the room to open so I could take a non-civil service test. *God, I couldn't work in a run-down building like this. I just had to get a job at the new turnpike building that was close to home and had parking.* But it was so political there. You had to "know" someone to get in. I sent letters to senators and congress members who responded with wonderful recommendations and directed me to this office for a test. *What if my hands shake for the typing part of the test? The phobia! God!*

The hall was empty *except* for a man who sang the words "Joy to the world" repeatedly with the emphasis on "joy" to a young girl. I surmise her name was Joy. It only worsened my glum mood.

A Corp was such a new beautiful building that was close to home with parking. These downtown state buildings are so old, and I would probably have to take a bus to work. *No! I did that for two years when I worked at the Telephone Company before A Corp. No! I was not doing that anymore! I could not work here.*

The test ended up being quite easy, although I was not sure of the typing part. I kept making mistakes and stopping to erase them. *It is okay!*

I told myself. They did say that we could take the typing test over if we didn't pass it.

I had taken the civil service test with excellent results the month before. Something like thirty people did better than me, and 300 did worse. I was sure to get interviews, but I was scared because I didn't want a state job. I only wanted to go back to A Corp. I didn't want to lose seventeen years' worth of service with five weeks of vacation and a good salary. I even called them for another job. Oh, they would take me back, alright. They told me I would have to go back to the accounting department. God, I couldn't do that. I begged the personnel department to place me in another department. They conveniently told me there was no job within the restrictions Dr. Ambrose placed on me. *God, what was wrong with me? Why did I need A Corp so much? I could not let go!*

The weather was dreadful. I could hardly walk back to the parking garage after the test, with the wind pushing me backward. My beautiful purple and black wool scarf blew off. I did not chase it. I only wanted to get to my safe home.

Time passed, and I did get many opportunities for state interviews. For the first couple of meetings, I was so nervous that my tongue stuck to the roof of my dry mouth. However, I got good at them. I might have even been hired if I wouldn't have sabotaged myself by saying, "I cannot tolerate stress." I wanted and needed a job, but I couldn't go back out there. Even with my candor, I did get a job offer, which I promptly turned down. And, the much-hoped-for call from the non-civil service turnpike administration never came. As I said, it was a "political" office.

CHAPTER 24

I Just Got the Job!

1993

I spent the next year in a daily routine of sleeping in, brunches of English muffins with apricot preserves, going to the dollar store with mom and walking up to the local cemetery in the afternoons. But the "job market" dried up. I was no longer getting interview availability notices for the state even though I took the civil service test once again. There was a hiring freeze. It didn't matter because my latest job aspiration was with the federal government.

I had run into an old acquaintance of my family during one of my mall window-shopping trips. Flo was doing exceptionally well at the Naval Depot. She was promoted and moving up in job grades. She was making more money than I was at A Corp. And, she didn't have a college degree either. I took the Federal employment test in February of 1993. Months went by, and I heard nothing until:

September 8, 1993

Today mom and I went to the mall. It is a rainy, dreary day—the first in a long time. It felt kind of good to put on sneakers, socks, and a sweatshirt today. I got a call at eight o'clock last night from Ms. Tina at a federal office to come in for an interview. My interview is at nine o'clock tomorrow morning.

Julija Rudolf

September 9, 1993

I had my interview this morning with the office manager. I believe she is going to hire me. I do. Bill said I'm "counting my chickens." He might be right. The interview just felt right to me. I am so excited about the whole thing. I believe I am ready to work again! It felt good to be behind a desk and typewriter for Ms. Tina's typing test. And, my hands didn't shake either! I know she is going to hire me!

September 23, 1993

I just got the job! Ms. Tina called me and told me that I got the job! They are having four new people come in. I start on Monday, October 4. Now I have to think about how I'm going to get there and back. Do I drive? Do I take a bus? Where do I park? God, I have to be able to work this job. Next week I think I'll go downtown to the parking garage by my new office and try to arrange for monthly parking. Lots to do in a week! I am so hyped!

October 4, 1993

I'm so tired on this my first day at work. But I survived it. I did. I hope I'm able to work it. I'm going to try. It's eight o'clock now. I made supper. I took my white Shepard, Sam, for a walk. I washed the dishes and ironed an outfit for tomorrow. I felt like something hot, so I made a cappuccino. I hope I can do the work. I was worried about that today. It looks complicated. I felt extraordinary stress, but I managed to hold onto it. The people seem like they will be patient. Everybody called me this evening—mom, Mike, and Catherine. I had an odd dream last night. It was about going to the highs and going to the lows (doing extremes) to escape something. It was strange. I don't remember everything.

October 5, 1993

I came home from work, really stressed out. I had a real hard time typing on the computer. The girl who trained me was not very good at teaching. I don't think she wanted to do it. She went through it quite fast, and I guess I'm supposed to know it. I shouldn't completely blame her. I am slow. I felt like leaving today. I am so stressed out. I came home, and I cried. I feel horrible. It's almost 8:30. I went to bed at nine last night. I don't know if I'm going to make it. Catherine thinks I should give it one month. I told her I would. Physically I feel bad. My legs hurt me from the stress. I feel like going to sleep right now. I'm going to make my lunch now.

October 7, 1993

Yesterday I was so stressed out. I came home and cried and cried until my eyelids swelled up. I was a mess—a real mess. Today went better. I called Dr. Ambrose last night and cried to him. He called in a prescription for me for a mild tranquilizer. They worked. I'm surprised he did that. But I wouldn't have made it any other way. I did better today. I went into Ms. Tina this morning and told her that I have schizophrenia, and I'm trying to work, but I don't know if I'll be able to. She was nice about that.

October 8, 1993

It's Friday, and I finally feel relaxed. It was a rough week. I didn't know if I was going to make it. I did! It's a small miracle considering the beginning of the week for me. I was seriously ready to quit that job. It's going to be a day by day thing, I believe. It's amazing how that one-half milligram of Ativan took the edge off the stress I was feeling, and I was able to start learning and understanding.

October 10, 1993

I feel like I am finally winding down from my stressful first week of work. God, it was so hard on me. I hope that when I go to see Dr. Ambrose on Saturday, he will increase the Pamelor so that I will not feel as stressed out. He said that would do it. I don't know how I made it through my first week of work. I almost didn't make it, and it's not over yet. I have to go day by day. I was thinking about how I told Ms. Tina, I had schizophrenia. I felt much shame thinking about that. I allowed myself to feel it. This is not easy for me. It just isn't. I feel like I want to buy work clothes, but I don't want to do that until I see if I'm going to be able to work. I hope I can do it. I want to be able to work. I do want to.

CHAPTER 25

The New Office

October 1993

When I was home on disability, I watched a talk show about a gentleman who was in a wheelchair. He was praising the administration in which I now worked. Oh, I so looked forward to a great office environment. I soon realized it was not exactly as he portrayed in the hearing office where I worked.

Three other women started work here the same day as I did. Joanne became a decision typist like me. She was at least ten years younger than me, and every other word out of her mouth was an expletive. She quickly caught onto the work. I was still trying to get myself together emotionally. With the kind computer technician's assistance, in time, I caught onto my job and was able to maintain the same "numbers" of decisions transcribed as Joanne. Some days my totals were higher. However, Joanne immediately got caught up in the office clique. She became Ms. Tina's favorite because of her new circle of friends. I call them the "old school staff." They were the people who had worked in the office since it's conception. Ms. Tina was "old school" as well.

I stayed very low-keyed. I didn't want trouble like I had at A Corp. I did make a friend there—my dear Elizabeth. Elizabeth was my age, very pretty, and quite intelligent. She moved to that office from Pittsburgh after her husband suddenly passed away, leaving her to raise two young sons. In her previous position with the administration, she was an office manager like Ms. Tina. Perhaps that was why Ms. Tina hated her so much. Elizabeth knew all the ins and outs of the hearing office. Maybe even more so than Ms. Tina. Ms. Tina perceived Elizabeth as a threat. One day, I came into the office, and Elizabeth's head rested on her typewriter as she sobbed. In Ms. Tina's eyes, Elizabeth could do nothing right. Even the "old school" clique was assisting Ms. Tina to find every "t" not crossed or "i" not dotted by Elizabeth. It was "dirty."

CHAPTER 26

"Old School" Politics

1994

I had come back from getting coffee and a homemade sticky bun from the café across the street. That was my new morning ritual. Unfortunately, those delicious pastries did nothing for my waistline. I couldn't help myself, though. Eating sugar was my new stress outlet. I needed an outlet. It was that, and the frequent smoke breaks at the ashtray outside by the front door that kept me sane, or so I thought.

Ms. Tina was in early that day. She announced that there would be a staff meeting at 10 AM. I was intrigued. But quickly after the meeting began, my mood was dashed.

Ms. Tina began, "I am presenting a recognition award to Joanne for her excellent work as a decision typist."

Everyone clapped, including me. *God, I did the same work and didn't get an award.* Although I worked harder to keep up, sometimes I even exceeded Joanne's numbers. I really didn't want to see the "old school" politics that were so prevalent in my new office. It was too soon after A Corp. I felt slighted and very disappointed. Still, I stayed under the radar. Quite unlike Jean Marie, who started working there the same day as me.

Jean Marie was young. This may have been her first job out of high school. Again, I stayed below the radar and didn't involve myself in office politics. For some reason, Ms. Tina began to pick on Jean Marie even though she was a fantastic docketing clerk. She was faster than anyone else in the entire office.

When Elizabeth was having problems, she went to Geraldine, the union steward, for help. Geraldine wasn't very reputable as she had her own emotional disorder. She was a compulsive liar. But to her credit, she kept Elizabeth from being fired when Ms. Tina was "out to get her."

And so, that is the route Jean Marie took. She went to Geraldine, who advised her to write a letter to Ms. Tina. Jean Marie wrote a letter asking Ms. Tina why she picked on her. I know all of this because Geraldine relayed this confidential Union business to the whole office.

I couldn't understand why Jean Marie would write this letter while she was still on probation. But she was young and inexperienced. Geraldine should have known better, though.

The letter Jean Marie presented to Ms. Tina didn't go over well at all. It went around the office that Jean Marie had until the end of the day to resign or be fired. Management did not need a reason as we were still on probation.

When I left the office at 3:00 PM after my work shift, I ran into Jean Marie in the parking garage. She was crying. I felt so badly for her.

I hugged her, "I'm so sorry."

"You *know*?" She half screamed at me.

I regretted that I said something to her. But the whole office knew what had transpired. That was the last time I saw Jean Marie.

CHAPTER 27

The Promotion

1994

My friend Elizabeth was a legal clerk. After talking to her one day at lunch, that became my goal as well. To achieve that position, you first had to put in your time as a hearing clerk. I so looked forward to a promotion. An announcement came out in the early spring of 1994, advertising two open hearing clerk positions in our office. I put in the proper paperwork, and it was accepted. Both Joanne and I were "moving up the ladder." I was to begin my new position as a hearing clerk with Judge Wright in July.

Samantha, Judge Wright's current clerk, was promoted to a legal clerk. That was the order of progression in the office. First, she was going to train me. I took many notes, and I made a binder for the procedures.

I worked hard to keep up with the demands of the job. I didn't even take the time to go across the street for a sticky bun. Instead, I brought in packs of wintergreen lifesavers and nervously chewed on them all day long. I'm sure Judge Wright saw how hard I worked to keep up, but he had no patience. He was always growling at me.

"When are you going to do my travel vouchers?" and "How many hearings did you set up for me now?" I soon realized just how full of themselves those judges were.

I felt some confidence in myself. *Damn, I AM going to be able to do this job!* It was short-lived. Ms. Tina called me into her office.

"We are getting a new Judge. Judge Gupta. You will be responsible for his work as well as Judge Wright's work beginning in September."

Oh, my God! My whole face fell in dismay. *I was just going to be alright with my job, and she's giving me another judge!*

I had no choice but to take on my new assignment. With Judges Wright and Gupta, my position as a hearing clerk, became quite impossible. Between the attorney calls, "I need an exhibit file copied," and the double amount of mail to be associated, I couldn't cope anymore. I was drowning in work with the only option to just keep moving. I felt the other hearing clerks watch me from their desks as if I was a sideshow act at a circus. One tumultuous day bled into the other.

November 4, 1994

It's Friday. I hate to say it, but I am in pain. I went to Burger King at lunch today. On my way out the door, I saw Paul and Ed, another credit manager from A Corp. I couldn't face them. I am fat, and I have my glasses on, and I don't look good. I got in the car, and I felt like I wanted to cry. I didn't, though. I felt like I wanted to hold Paul and Ed and say, "Look what happened to me." I feel pain most of the time. I feel pain about my work. Years have gone by, and I have not recovered from everything that happened to me. I feel so bad. I can't take it back. It happened, and I have to go on with my life. I still haven't accepted that I lost my job at A Corp. I still haven't accepted that. I had brief suicidal thoughts. Nothing serious. I didn't dwell on it. Please, God, help me to recover. I want to cry, and I can't.

November 10, 1994

I had a bad day today. I took an Ativan and regrouped at lunch. I'm going to have to start putting in some credit hours in order to do my scheduling.

Damn. Today we had a meeting, and we were told that we are going to have to release our own cases. It is impossible for me to do all the work I have now. I cannot take on more. I have made up my mind that I am seriously looking for another job. I am doing that. Tomorrow I am getting up at 5:30 AM. I will drink my coffee, take a shower, and fill out my applications for the State. Then I will take the test. And if need be, I can join their clerical pool. I will update my resume too. At least I will be doing something positive about this horrible situation I am in. Today Judge Gupta said that we were treated like slave labor. He used to work for the Equal Employment Opportunity Commission. I hate my job. I am getting out of there. I am concerned about having to buy benefits. And the money I will have to spend on my medications. I should take an afternoon off and go to an employment agency to get a job as well. I must make every effort I can now. I will. I feel positive about this.

CHAPTER 28

The Options

November 12, 1994

The shrill buzz of my alarm went through me like a shockwave. It was early in the morning, and I had nightmares all night. It was Saturday, but I had an appointment. I always counted down the days until I saw the most important person in my life then—Dr. Ambrose. *Surely today is the day he will deliver me from my pain and suffering. Today is the day of the miracle—he will heal me.*

But alas, it wasn't that way at all. The doctor's wife was very ill, and his mind was consumed with his own troubles. For me, it was like someone hit me over the head with a hammer. For the first time since 1986, I came to realize that I was the only one who could help myself. It was all on me. The doctor was human. Not some God-like being who performed miracles. I felt so alone.

But in his way, Dr. Ambrose did do well by me that day. After my lamentations, the good doctor asked, "Julija, what are your options?"

He went on in his logical manner, "You can look for another job, but in the meantime, go back to a decision typist."

He was right!

Sunday came and went.

November 14, 1994

Monday. I was more nervous than usual. I couldn't wait for Ms. Tina to arrive. As soon as she did, I asked if I could talk to her. I couldn't take the pressure any longer. I had to get this over with.

Before I knew it, I was seated before this office manager in her little corner office.

"Ms. Tina," I stammered, "I need to go back to a decision typist. My doctor thinks that is the best thing for me to do." I held my breath.

"You know, Julija, once I took a job that I didn't like, and I stepped back to what I was before."

Oh, the relief I felt at that. The stress immediately drained from me.

Ms. Tina went on, "You can apply for a hearing clerk again in the future if you choose to."

Was I making a mistake? I haven't felt right since July, I argued neurotically with myself.

Well, as Dr. Ambrose said, at least I have a job, and maybe I could work on getting something different. *There is so much the future could have in store for me!*

CHAPTER 29

Hearing Clerk Once Again

1996

Another year passed, and I became proficient as a decision typist. However, it was not the career I wanted for the next twenty years. I was reduced to a grade five on the pay scale. The legal clerks were grade eights, and their only work involved making medical records into an official exhibit file. I needed that job. I could "taste" it.

One summer day, I was surprised when Joanne announced that she was leaving our office for a new position with the State. She had given Ms. Tina her resignation letter that morning. *Oh, so that's why Ms. Tina was crying.* I never did understand the "old school" office dynamics. An announcement for a hearing clerk opened. Once again, I thought I would try to acquire and work in this position. It was the pathway to becoming a legal clerk. So, I submitted my application, and it was accepted.

My new position as a hearing clerk was primarily with Judge Gupta. However, I did schedule hearings for Judge Polanski as well. His hearings were held in Charlotte, North Carolina.

Even with the extra judge, I was able to maintain the workload due to new computer automation. The days passed by quickly. But my bubble burst when Judge Gupta told me that he was transferring to the Baltimore office. We worked so well together. He must have thought that, too, because he asked me if I would be interested in moving to the Baltimore office with him. I was flattered, of course, but I could never leave my close-knit family. My only assignment now was Judge Polanski. I had free time, but I spent it helping Dale, the hearing clerk who worked for Judge Luther, who generated an excessive amount of paperwork.

For me, this was the ideal job. For one thing, Dale and I were stationed in the office annex. No one worked in that office but the four of us (and sometimes the two Reading Judges.) I was so proud of myself for how well I was doing.

There was talk that the Reading office would be made permanent, and, once again, Judge Polanski asked me to work with him at that location. I graciously declined.

Little did I know, change was in the wind. We were getting a new Chief Judge.

CHAPTER 30

Either I Like You or I Don't

1997

Flamboyant! That's the only way that I can describe our new copper-haired Chief Judge who blew into our office like a whirlwind. Judge Rita Sweitzer wasted no time demonstrating her tyrannical rule. First, I was assigned to Judge Luther, the high producer who I helped Dale with. Secondly, we were moving to the new office tower next to the city hall. To my dismay, the judges were to increase their number of hearings held each month from thirty-five to sixty. *God, here I go once again-more scheduling, more post, more of everything! I'm not going to be able to keep up. I have no choice but to hang in there until I can promote to a legal clerk. Hopefully, that will be soon.* I was next in line to be the next hearing clerk promoted to a legal clerk according to past office progression.

My first official meeting with Judge Luther came shortly after we were settled into our new worksite. I began taking copious notes as he gave me his administrative details.

"My hearings will be scheduled for 9 o'clock, 10 o'clock, 12:30, at 1 o'clock, 2 o'clock and 3 o'clock."

I wrote down all the details in my notebook. The judge ended his dictation with a warning to me. At least that's what it felt like.

"Either I like you, or I don't like you," he bluntly stated.

I explicitly obeyed his instructions and immediately began to set up his schedule.

The first day of the hearings that I scheduled soon arrived. Dutifully, I carried the cases, itinerary, and vendor vouchers into his office for him to review. It wasn't long before he called for me.

"Now who would set up a hearing for 12:30?" he drilled angrily.

"But you gave me that time," I meekly stated.

I went to my desk and got out my notebook to show this Judge. He looked at my scribbled notes, but I could see he was not going to take the blame. No, it was on me. This judge considered himself perfect. Now I knew which side of the "either I like you, or I don't," coin was flipped. The next year proved me right.

Judge Luther was not one to hide his disfavor of a person. And he didn't with me. It was no secret that my work was backed up. But Judge Luther didn't make it any easier when he stood over my shoulder and rifled through my mail and the files on my desk while I worked.

Then came the day his wife visited our office. He took her around the office, making introductions to the staff, but he avoided my cubicle altogether. I was shunned. I felt so lowly and worthless, and I blamed myself.

Release was finally mine when I requested a six-week job detail to a legal clerk through the union, and it was approved.

After a brief training session, I began my detail as a legal clerk. I worked it with my whole heart. I had to show management how efficiently I could do the job. I worked up forty cases in one month. I was the second-highest case puller out of all the legal clerks when I turned in my monthly report. I did other duties as well. I was good.

Usually, when you work a detail, management gave a recognition award. I received none of that when my detail ended. No "Atta girl." Nothing. It was getting progressively harder to come to work anymore. It was burnout.

CHAPTER 31

The Job Announcement

November 1997

What a day I picked to work the later shift. I missed all the early-morning office buzz when Mark, my fellow hearing clerk, found an open announcement for a legal clerk on the administration's website. *Why wasn't the announcement posted in our office? It was for our office.* It should have been published with all the other open announcements. I went to our regional Union Vice President, and he looked as well. The announcement was not there.

Nonetheless, I got all the particulars of Announcement No. 555–555 on the internet, and I was going to put in my application for legal clerk. There were two open positions, so surely one was mine. I was so excited. Finally, I was going to be a legal clerk. I was getting away from pompous Judge Luther.

Alas, something good was in the wind. I was going through a rather bad time at work and at home. I had a new psychiatrist who was experimenting with different psychotropic medications. However, I knew what the real problem was. It was the stressful office environment. My only hope was to be promoted to a legal clerk.

The holidays came and went, and still no word. I was anxious as I was having a tough time.

Julija Rudolf

February 6, 1998

Today I started taking Wellbutrin as an antidepressant. I take one pill in the morning. I feel really odd. My face burns. There were times today that I felt like I was going to lose it. And times that I thought I would pass out. Wellbutrin is the same drug that they are using to help people quit smoking. I have a dull headache that I think is the result of the pill. I was useless at work today. We had our stress management meeting this morning at work. Wow! Everybody spoke up about how much stress there is in our office. Well, almost everybody—not the goody-two-shoes. Today I told my immediate supervisor that I needed help with my work. She helped me. I felt much better when it was time to leave. I am so glad it's Friday. That gives my body two days to get used to this new pill. I feel shaky inside right now.

CHAPTER 32

The New Hire

February 10, 1998

I froze dead in my tracks after I swiped my badge and opened the office door this morning. *My God! Who is that strange man with ponytailed hair sitting with the legal clerks?* The official procedure binders were scattered around his desk! I signed in and walked to my desk in a daze. *What? Did they hire a new legal clerk? Who is that man? My God, I was next in line for that job!*

I had no time to think about this. Jill, one of the supervisors, gave me a list of cases that she wanted cleared up by February 12, 1998. Then shortly after Jill's directives, Peggy, the other supervisor, called me. She wanted the FPM cases scheduled, and notices sent. And, to top it all off, Judge Luther wanted the cases for the ninth scheduled and mailed by February 12, 1998. But what I really needed to do was associate notices and do invoices for Tuesday's hearings by Thursday, February 11. They hit me all at once. I was so stressed that my chest hurt me. *Is that what they wanted? Did they want to make me sick like they did at A Corp? Are they doing this to me on purpose? And, who is that man sitting with the legal clerks?* My head spun. It was time to pay a visit to Art, the Union Vice President.

I wasted no time heading to his office. I didn't go to the downstairs offices too often, but that day, I half-think Art was expecting me.

"What can I do for you?" Art cordially asked. I do believe he already knew why I was paying him a visit.

"Is it what it looks like?" I simply inquired.

"I believe so, Julija. It looks like they hired someone to fill the open announcement." Art matter-of-factly responded.

"I can't believe it." I went on, "Mark and I both felt that we would be promoted. There were two openings, you know. Why Judge Sweitzer just told me that she enjoys working with me. And Ms. Tina told me I was an asset to the department. Then they didn't promote me? It doesn't make any sense!"

"I will check into it," Art stated. "I'll get back to you tomorrow, Julija."

I went home drained that evening.

February 11, 1998

After another sleepless night, I literally drug myself into the office the next morning. I planned to give Art a little time to drink his coffee before I planted myself in the chair in front of his desk.

Something was different. When I came into the office, I saw the new guy, whose name was Toby, leisurely sipping his coffee at his desk. Here I was under a slew of work directives and pulling eight inches of mail out of my "IN" box. I made up my mind right then, and there, I was not going to let all that work bother me anymore. I was just going to do one thing at a time. I was angry. But God, I was so burned out and defeated.

Before I had a chance to march downstairs, Art came up to my desk. He gave me a copy of the letter he wrote to Ms. Tina, asking her for the particulars of the new hire. Art said it put her on notice that a grievance might be filed. But more importantly, Ms. Tina told Art that Toby's name was the only name on the new hire list. *How can that be? I applied on the*

Open Continuous Announcement and on the Administration's Temporary Announcement for Legal Clerk. What was going on? Didn't my name make the lists?

No sooner had Art left, and I was on the phone with the personnel department. I found out that my name made it to both lists. What was Ms. Tina talking about when she told Art that the new legal clerk, Toby was the only name on the list? *I am so angry! I'm going to fight this. I will write a letter to my congressman. I may file an EEOC complaint. And I am really going to try to not be stressed at work. It isn't worth it. Look what they are doing to me.*

February 18, 1998

Today was the first day I took Zoloft. It's 8:45 PM, and it's my first chance to relax all day. I feel very strange right now—like I could lose it. It must be all the chemicals in my body. Wellbutrin is probably still with me. I can hardly see to write as my vision is so blurred. I wore my reading glasses most of today. It might be my medication. I have a headache right now. I felt so much stress at work that by the end of the day, my chest hurt me. I don't even feel like getting up to light the kerosene heater. Tomorrow I have to type up a letter to Personnel requesting information on the legal clerk position that was filled. I have to call the Employee Assistance Program (EAP) to get an appointment with a counselor.

February 23, 1998

I am very depressed again. I know I need more Zoloft. The doctor is going to double my dose on my next appointment. Work is horrible. I am having a bad time. I don't know what I am going to do. I can't think right now. I took an Ativan. At work many times today, I wanted to cry. I wanted to leave there. Last Friday, Judge Luther told me that if I don't schedule his cases, he won't be able to cover for me, and it will come down on me. I felt so bad. At work today, I told Peggy that I couldn't keep up with Judge Luther. My work was behind. I felt like I was going to have a nervous breakdown. Of course,

I didn't tell Peggy that. I feared she would use it against me. But I do feel like I could lose it. I can't wait until Monday for my doctor's appointment. He can up my dose of Zoloft. I can tell him that I feel like I'm going to have a nervous breakdown. Judge Luther is a little easier to get along with than he had been at first. I haven't been this depressed since 1990 and 1991. God, I was through so much.

CHAPTER 33

The Performance Review

March 11, 1998

I couldn't get myself to go into the office the day before. I didn't want to go at all, but alas, I needed to pay my respects to my outlandish workload!

"Good morning, Mark," I greeted him as I passed by his cubicle situated next to mine.

Mark immediately ran over to my desk.

"Julija," he whispered breathlessly, "Toby was a used car salesman from outside of the government, and he didn't even have veteran's preference."

Of course, I was taken aback by the news. I was glad I filed that grievance. I wanted to know why I wasn't considered. They had until March 12 to respond, and I was going to have it bumped up to higher union management. I considered taking it to the EEOC (Equal Employment Opportunity Commission) if I was not satisfied. I would have to say that they passed me up because I had a disability. Both Mark and I should've gotten those jobs. There was only one vacancy left. *Will they give it to one of us, or are they waiting to give it to someone else from outside?* I was furious because, for the past five years or so, I worked like a fool for that promotion.

And that's the way it went that day, feeling anger, then depression, then anger again. It was like mood swings. And finally, I went numb. At least I have a doctor's appointment tomorrow, so I get to leave early.

The next day proved a whole lot easier going into work as I was leaving the office at 1 o'clock. But once again, I had a surprise in store for me. Today Jill called me into her office. *God! What now?*

"It's time for your review," Jill stated as she motioned for me to take a seat.

It's that time so soon? I questioned myself. It was all so odd. And what made it even weirder is that she tried to get me to talk about the grievance I filed. I didn't bite. But she wasn't giving up.

"Is there anything you want to talk about?"

"No," I responded.

Bound and determined to get me to "talk," she said, "It's just the usual stress then? I understand Peggy is helping you with some things."

"Yes, scheduling."

"Incidentally," I finally spoke up, "I got Judge Luther's rocket docket done in record time. I came up with a new procedure for getting the notices completed quickly—very fast indeed."

I went into significant detail to Jill as I thought my idea would benefit all the hearing clerks. But she wasn't the least bit interested.

Then I asked her if she could help me complete a leave slip for Friday.

"I have a doctor's appointment in the morning and an appointment with an EAP counselor in the afternoon."

God, you would think she just sucked a lemon! I fought back a smile to see the look on her face at the mention of the EAP. Those EAP people are kept "informed" by quite a few of the hearing office staff those days. I was anxious to sit down with my new counselor soon!

CHAPTER 34

The EAP Appointment

March 13, 1998

Strong. Compassionate. Authoritative. As a nine-year-old child, that is how I felt about Ben, the 15-year-old leading character of Rob White's book, *The Lion's Paw*. In fact, that character's traits struck me so profoundly that I penciled a little blurb from the book into my childhood scrapbook.

I saw my EAP counselor, Dr. James, for the first time. After introductions and pleasantries, I could only liken this handsome, state police psychologist, to my childhood hero, Ben. My appointment was very timely, indeed. After informing Dr. James of the office intricacies, I continued.

"Dr. James, yesterday, Mark and I got an answer to our grievance." I began. "Mark and I were on the list for promotion to a legal clerk. There were two vacancies to fill. However, through our grievance, we found out that there was some obscure announcement that neither Mark nor I were aware of. It was only announced on the internet and the office of personnel management's employment telephone number. It was for a temporary legal clerk position. It was announcement No. 00-001. I applied for Announcement No. 555-555, and that was also a temporary position for legal clerk, which was posted on the Administration's site. Why choose someone from Announcement No. 00-001 who is not qualified, instead of someone from Announcement No. 555-555 who was well qualified? They both were for the same position."

Dr. James was sympathetic. I do believe he saw the truth even before I did. Ms. Tina and Judge Sweitzer simply didn't want to promote me. They were employing all kinds of underhanded methods to avoid doing so. I questioned if Judge Sweitzer knew Toby before-hand and clued him in. I would not put anything past them!

"Julija, you have six free visits with the EAP." Dr. James said. "I would like to continue to see you. I accept your insurance, and I waive what you owe for a deductible. You need not pay me anything out of your pocket."

And so, began years of Dr. James' guidance and protection. During my time seeing this good doctor, he saved my marriage when Bill had another DUI; and my job when I had a psychotic break in 2003. He indeed was a "helper."

CHAPTER 35

Plea for Help

March 22, 1998

Dear Congressman Olley:

Working conditions in our office are appalling. I cannot believe my job is in the United States of America. I cannot begin to tell you how many people in our office are on medication for depression. Also, I have been referred by the Employee Assistance Program to see a counselor for stress due to this dreadful workplace. My counselor tells me that he is seeing five people from my office, and he knows of three others who are going to other counselors. The EAP people have been to our office on two occasions. Once, for a stress management meeting, which turned into a plea for help from my fellow employees. And on the second occasion, to speak to employees on a one-to-one basis. I cannot stress the deplorable working conditions enough. Four people, including myself, have recently filed complaints with the EEOC. The whole problem is the Chief Judge, Rita Sweitzer, and the Hearing Manager, Ms. Tina. Something must be done. The middle working-class people are the backbone of this country. In my office, we are treated like slaves. All they want from us are "numbers," which they "fudge" for Congress anyway. And all at the expense of the normal worker, like myself. We do have some people who Judge Sweitzer seems to favor. It has caused a hostile division in our office that has never been there before. How can you have teamwork and service the public when you have conditions like this? It is Sunday evening, and I will probably have nightmares about work again tonight. Please investigate the situation in the Office of Hearings. Thank you for your time and consideration.

I sealed, stamped, and placed my letter in the mailbox receptacle the next morning. It was done.

October 8, 1998

Today I went to a going-away luncheon for Mark. He is going out on Medical Retirement because of stress. I have worked in the Hearing Office for five years as of October 3ʳᵈ. It was a successful work attempt by me after being on Social Security Benefits myself for three years. I am Bipolar. It was not easy for me to go back to work after being psychotic for a year and a half solid. I worked hard to get myself together again and pick up the pieces of my life. But I did it.

1999

The next year or so filled my flowered pocket calendar with EEO deadlines and meetings with my attorney (which incidentally, I paid thousands of dollars for, while management used the Administration's attorneys free of charge). But I had a cause, and even strait-laced judge Luther sympathized with me.

CHAPTER 36

The Promotion

2000

Y2K. That became a familiar acronym in 1999. 2000 was feared to be the year that confused computers worldwide. The doomsday sayers just knew the year changeover from 1999 to 2000 would cripple banks, satellites, and even our electrical grid. At least, that was the prominent topic of conversation.

For me, 2000 was more of the same; work overload and management mind games. *And the stress at home, God, how did I survive the stress at home?* I was responsible for everything. It was way out of control. Not to mention, living with an active alcoholic. I don't know how I survived.

I thought I would finally see the light of day when Judge Sweitzer called Renée, the master docket clerk, and myself into her office. It could only mean one thing, and I had the biggest grin on my face. But it was only out of nervousness.

I felt her abhorrence when Judge Sweitzer made her announcement to us.

"Congratulations, Renée and Julija, you are both being promoted to a legal clerk."

Judge Schweitzer always liked Renée. However, I knew that she had no choice but to promote me. I made too much of a stink, especially with the congressmen I was in contact with. Oh, I do believe upper management and regional headquarters had something to do with my promotion. No matter, I was going to be a legal clerk in the year 2000.

Well, it all seemed too hard to believe. But as it turned out, 2000 brought more changes to our office in the form of a new initiative called OEP or Office Efficiency Program.

With these new procedures, the legal clerks basically took on the same duties as hearing clerks, as well as pulling exhibit files. And they expected higher "numbers" of cases pulled as well as the hearing duties. *Was this a cruel joke?* Thank heavens for my psychologist, Dr. James.

CHAPTER 37

Perjury

2001

On my way up Simpson Avenue for my appointment with Dr. James, my mind traveled back in time. Years flashed back, further still, until I saw myself seated in the familiar black recliner in Doctor Andrews' office. 1986 once again, and I was deep in a hypnotic trance.

Entranced. Frightened. I saw myself hiding behind the old wooden planks of a barn wall.

My breath quickened.

Sitting in the black recliner in Dr. Andrews' office, I was caught up in the life of Marie Chambre.

"I'm hiding," I tensely told Dr. Andrews.

"Who are you hiding from?"

"Shhhh! They'll hear you!" I whispered in annoyance.

"The soldiers are coming," I continued between labored breaths as I peered through the crack in the wall.

"Why are you hiding from the soldiers?" He probed, "I thought the soldiers were good."

"They're government!" I exclaimed with a quickness. "The government is corrupt!"

I was irritated by the doctor because he questioned me about the soldiers. He should have already known the government was corrupt. It certainly was instinctively clear to me as I relived the event from the black recliner. I saw a young boy in the yard. A soldier was talking to him.

"He's slapping him," I frantically whispered as the soldier hit the child's face with his open hand.

That was where the trance ended in 1986. A car horn beeping at me to go when the light turned green, brought me back to Simpson Avenue and 2001.

That particular hypnosis session in 1986 hit home with me. The story I told under trance back then seemed too real to be my imagination. Maybe it was real. Maybe the government was corrupt. Afterall, I was going to tell Dr. James all about my EEO hearing that transpired last week. Seated in his "library" office surrounded by shelves of marvelous books, I told Dr. James of my daydream on my way there.

"I know the origin of reliving the past hypnotic trance, Dr. James," I continued. "And the government IS corrupt!"

"Julija," Dr. James said, "We talked extensively about your EEO hearing so you would be prepared for it.

"I want to thank you for your encouragement, but I wasn't prepared for an outright lie!" I spit out.

"Dr. James, Ms. Tina lied under oath. She perjured herself when the judge asked her if the announcement Toby was hired from was posted in my office. She said that it was. She said, 'Yes.'" I woefully recalled.

Dr. James didn't say any more to that. What could he say?

And then, to my dismay, a couple of months after that appointment, I got the EEOC judge's decision in the mail. I held my breath and opened the brown envelope. The first sentence told the story. I read the word, "Unfavorable," and I knew right then and there that I lost my EEO case. I lost the thousands of dollars I paid to my attorney. What's worse, I lost my enthusiasm even though I was finally a legal clerk in the Hearing office. Nothing mattered anymore. I stopped cooking and cleaning. But worst of all, I stopped my lifeline of journaling. I shutdown.

CHAPTER 38

The Buddhist Priest

2005

I was in a mental cocoon for several years, where I lived with a twenty-four-hour neurotic desire to quit smoking. It consumed my attention, a vicious merry-go-round to nowhere. I needed the spark of something that wasn't counting cigarettes and especially wasn't work. After all, they both failed me. I didn't know it, but I was about to be in the right place at the right time.

The weather was dreary and gray, so I decided to just walk across the street for lunch at the food court in the community center. A double bonus: yummy pizza and a religion fair that had been advertised that week. I loved religion; all the denominations. I picked up a copy of the Koran, as well as the Talmud. I had gathered quite a collection of pamphlets when, there in the corner of the floor, I saw a rather stoic looking young man handing out business cards. I graciously accepted one that read, "Mindfulness Counseling." I was intrigued. When I went back to the office, I called the number on the card. I didn't know what to expect, but a kindly woman answered and explained the workings of the Buddhist Society on Cedar Road.

Before I knew it, I was seated in the local Buddhist dojo awaiting my first appointment with Sensei Earl. The tall, stately gentleman in jeans and sandals who came out to collect me was not what I anticipated a Buddhist priest to look like. Sensei Earl was a regular person.

He motioned me to the sofa in a nook of his office where his spiritual table was set up. The smell of incense filled the air. I began my first of many lessons in his unique mindfulness study.

For me, it was a lot to grasp. My mind was always in a state of turmoil. But it was the spark I needed for my own spiritual awakening. Dr. Andrews once told me, "Sometimes, all you need is for someone to plant a seed." As Sensei Earl dictated the lessons, I took notes in my blank journal. It was a seed planted! And so, I began to journal once again.

Besides Dr. James, I could feel Sensei cared about me. He never failed me. Even when I came to him rambling in psychosis, he didn't "disown" me.

And when it wasn't Sensei, it was another teacher at the dojo. It was JC and then finally, Patrick. Yes, Patrick was special indeed.

CHAPTER 39

Hypnosis Once Again

2005

About the same timeframe as I was visiting the dojo, Dr. James was planning his retirement from the state police and his move to Florida. I decided to use the yellow pages once again. "Hypnosis," I searched, "Smoking Cessation," the ad read. I was going to try hypnosis. I found the person I needed to see, a psychologist named Brad. Oh, but he was going to have his work cut out for him! I had smoked since I was sixteen years old. God, I went to many Novenas to the Blessed Mother asking for a miracle.

"Please help me to quit smoking," I begged Her on my knees.

I was fifty-three years old and smoking one super-slim after the other. I tried everything, patches, non-nicotine cigarettes, and pills.

During the first session with my new psychologist, we did a preliminary interview.

"Do you have any experience with hypnosis?" This handsome gentleman asked me as he had me follow his flashlight on the wall with my eyes.

"Why, yes, I do!" I exclaimed.

I told him of my fantastic sessions with Dr. Andrews, and about the French nurse, Marie Chambre. And, I told him of the spiritual trance with dad and with the Mother of God.

I had his attention. He was quite interested in "my gift," as Dr. Andrews called my hypnotic abilities.

The following week was my first hypnotic trance with Brad. I went into a deep "sleep" quite easily with the soothing tone of his voice.

"Now, see yourself on an escalator going deeper, deeper relaxed."

He went into his smoking cessation program. And when my time was up, he counted down.

"Five-four-three-two-one," he brought me back to reality.

I was awake and felt refreshed. But alas, I couldn't wait to light up that cigarette.

CHAPTER 40

The Devil and the Cigarettes

2005

The bright orange light of my alarm clock startled me as I sat straight up in the bed. 3 AM. My pajamas were soaked again. *Another nightmare!* This time the man in a black-hooded cloak reached the front door. When I first saw him, he was at the neighbor's huge pine tree. Closer. Closer every night in my frightening dreams. But tonight, he was here. He was at the door that I struggled to reach in time to turn the latch to lock.

I had seen the hooded man before. *When? When did I see him?* My mind drifted back in time. Back to my 1988 visit to the village of miracles–Medjugorje.

October 14, 1988

"Father, will you show me how to say the rosary?" I asked the young priest in Medjugorje.

We were standing on the portico of a little stone church waiting to go inside.

That day was special to me. I had seen the Blessed Mother the night before, and I felt so loved. It had been a while since I prayed the rosary. I wasn't sure of the order of the Our Father's and Glory Be's. But the priest only wanted to go inside to hear Father Leon's sermon. I was used to rejection, so I followed him in and sat in the seat that mom saved for me next to her.

Father Leon was supposedly a famous priest in the Medjugorje story. But he may as well have stabbed me in the heart that day with his lecture to a church full of worshipers.

He began his sermon with, "The devil is with you when you smoke."

My face flushed. I smoked. I saw the Blessed Mother the night before, and I smoked.

"You can't smoke and pray." he continued for the next hour.

I was painfully embarrassed. I had tried to quit smoking many times before. Was I evil?

I got angry. God, how could he tell me I was evil? His whole lecture was on the ills of smoking and the devil.

I can't help but think how the young priest I met on the portico, and I would have both benefited from saying the rosary together instead of going inside to listen to that hideous sermon.

My mind returned to the present as I pulled out a fresh set of PJs. Another sleepless night ahead, so I retrieved my dojo journal from the nightstand, and I wrote:

"I am depressed and in pain. I can't pray. I am in pain—mental pain. So, Father Leon is the devil with me now too? You judged me before. I didn't judge you even when I read on the Internet that they suspended you. I don't feel good. I binged on sugar. I was so upset. You know those of us who are too sick to pray are the poor souls in purgatory. Those of us who smoke because we are in pain, can't pray. So, Father Leon, you said you couldn't smoke and pray because the devil is with you. Is the devil with those in mental anguish then? All my life, my mission was to please people, but you said, back in 1988, that the devil was with me. Do you know how hard it is to please everyone all the

time? You know, Father, the Priesthood comes with a certain power. I believe that power can become a quest for glory for some Priests. Take care that you don't betray the true mission of Christ."

St. Elijah! I dropped my pen. I remembered where I saw the black-hooded figure. It was in Father Leon's church. It was a statue by the alter. It was the statue of St. Elijah with a raven that I saw in my dreams.

CHAPTER 41

The Subconscious Childhood Memory

2005

Brad was quite adept with hypnosis and was a member of the American Society of Clinical Hypnosis (ASCH). He had a unique procedure that put me into an intense trance.

"Feel the chair under you. Feel those sensations. Now see yourself on an escalator, going deeper and deeper."

It was another blessed hypnotic sleep to relieve my daily struggles; release from the pain of reality. During our first several months working together, Brad usually spent most of the hour in cigarette cessation techniques, but that changed.

That day, there was a break in his usual lecture. There was a period of silence where I cried out in a childlike voice.

"Stop, mommy, stop!"

I consciously heard Brad reel around in his leather chair. He wasn't expecting that outburst. Neither was I. I continued as if in auto-play. I was a child again.

"Stop, mommy! I can't breathe!" over and over in my mind. "Stop, mommy!"

She held both of my hands above my head. She kept slapping my face, slapping me repeatedly until I saw myself lying on the red and yellow tile kitchen floor. It was like I was somehow there, but no longer in my body. I was floating above myself, and I saw our neighbor lady at the screen door. I can still envision that yellow porch light illuminating the night outside.

"You didn't have to beat her," the woman quipped through the screen.

In trance, I saw myself, a child, traveling through a dark tunnel. People enveloped me in the blackness. I was in shock and extremely frightened. Then, I saw a light.

"Go back. Go back." a voice whispered.

I imagined the neighbor placed a wet towel on my forehead because the next thing I experienced was a cold, wet sensation. I was back in my body. My mother was crying.

Then, I heard the woman proclaim, "She's okay now."

"I made mommy cry," I muttered in dismay to Brad.

God, I made my mommy cry. I blamed myself. I went to hide between the refrigerator and the stove.

"Don't tell your dad, or he won't like you," mom told me.

I was completely worn down and broken. I didn't even cry.

"I wanna go to bed now."

My head sank to my shoulder, signaling the end of the session.

Brad directed, "When you are ready, count back from five to one. When you reach one, you will be awake and refreshed."

Even though I had no conscious memory of what I had relived for Brad, I did remember what led to that unfortunate event.

On a warm summer night, mom, the neighbor, and I were in our back yard admiring the beautiful view I grew up with; the river and valley below. The blue lights of the airport runway were twinkling across the way.

"Mommy, you stink," I startled her.

It was a perspiration odor. I got no response.

I repeated it, "Mommy, you stink."

I thought I was funny. She probably lovingly said the same thing to me when I was a baby in a soiled diaper. But instead of evoking laughter, she grabbed me by my arm and dragged me through the narrow pathway into the kitchen door at the back of the house.

"You embarrassed me!" she spits out between a clenched jaw.

I was extremely fatigued from what I experienced in trance. But it needed to "come out." I must find a way to heal.

CHAPTER 42

Dissociation

August 15, 2005

I go to see Brad tomorrow. I have been experiencing flashbacks of hiding behind the house while mom and dad fought. I remember staring at the faucet, which seemed larger than life. I want to do hypnosis on that thought, and the anticipation is filling me with dread. I pray to the Mother of God. I want it to be a productive session. But I fear what I might find out.

August 16, 2005

From the recliner in Brad's office, I saw raindrops patter on the window overlooking a delightful garden. With the tranquility, I went into trance quite smoothly, once again, to relive a memory from childhood. I had told my psychologist of my conscious memory from when I was probably five years old. The recollection of my parent's loud argument, and then the intent focus on a larger than life faucet knob always seemed odd to me.

Once in a deep sleep, I came up in a trance in mom's kitchen. She was cooking. Suddenly, all hell broke loose. Dad came through the door.

Mom screamed, "You son-of-a-bitch, where were you?"

I welled up with unbearable fear. She went after him with a knife. Screaming at each other, he ran into the bathroom and locked the door. She ran after him pounding on the door with the knife.

Dad, dad! I couldn't breathe! I ran out of the house and hid behind it by the cellar steps. My arms and legs went numb like they were dismembered from my body.

Brad inquired, "First thoughts. What are you thinking?"

"She's going to kill him." I blurted out. My situation was totally out of control. I mentally fled.

"I'm flying," I told Brad. "I'm flying above the trees. I'm as light as air. I'm flying with the birds." I laughed. "They're taking me for a ride. I can see the treetops."

My adult self interjected, "I've seen this before."

It was quiet. I couldn't hear the screaming anymore. *Oh, God. Oh, God.*

I reported, "I see the faucet. It wasn't there, but now it is. I am feeling emotional pain so great. It's like negative energy."

"Julija, Julija," mom was calling me.

I must go in. I don't want to.

Brad prodded, "First thoughts."

"I know dad's hurt. I know it. I have to go in."

But, dad's not here. Where's a dad?

Mom ordered, "Sit down and eat."

I just sat there and couldn't bear to eat. Mom went outside.

She came in and pulled me away from the table. She pushed me, and I went into the parlor and sat on the couch. I sat there, afraid to move. Finally, sleep overcame my troubled mind.

My head sank to my shoulder, and Brad brought me back to the present.

"Julija," Brad comforted me, "what you experienced at five is called dissociation. Something traumatic happened. You were completely helpless to control the situation. It was life-threatening."

"I felt like I left my body, Brad. God. I felt outside of my body."

Instead of stories of the French Nurse, it was me coming to life as a child again. *How do I deal with all of this? Tell me how?*

CHAPTER 43

The Confession

2005

I was mentally tormented likely because I couldn't forgive myself for my teenage promiscuity, or was it my little cousin, Emma's death? Some days were worse than others. On a scale of one to ten, I was a ten, and I needed absolution.

I walked down to the Cathedral during my lunch hour.

"Bless me, Father, for I have sinned."

In anguish and despair, I confessed to the Priest, "There is evil in me."

The pain of hearing myself say this in the dark confessional quaked my body. However, there was no consolation or comfort for me there. The Priest could not understand what it was that I needed. Maybe it was because I couldn't tell him what I needed.

He questioned, "Who told you that you were evil?"

God, God, I needed comfort. God, why did he say that? Was it true? Was I evil?

I left the church still a ten on that one to ten scale.

In desperation, I called my Buddhist counselor, Patrick. Later that day, it was he who gave me a reason to hold on. Once again seated on the sofa in the corner of his office, I felt his humanity. He was warm and cared about me. I was able to "confess."

1957

I was five years old the day, my little cousin, Emma, was visiting mom with Aunt Ellen. Emma was playing in our front yard. I went into mom's kitchen drawer and pulled out a piece of wax paper. Back outside with the paper between my tiny fingers, I pulled off a branch of sumac leaves from a bush growing in the cellar window vent. I gave it to my little cousin, and I told her to eat it. I ran. I don't believe she would have eaten leaves from a tree. I never knew if she did or didn't ingest them.

Days passed, and I forgot all about what I did to Emma until one day, I heard a worried Aunt Theresa tell my mom, "Emma got her lip caught on the screen door, and it wouldn't stop bleeding."

Oh no! My child's mind nagged. *I did that to her! It was my fault!* But what terrified me the most, *they're going to find out it was my doing!*

The next memory of Emma was this tiny child in a beautiful white dress lying in her coffin in Aunt Ellen's parlor. My cousins and I counted a multitude of flowers as the steady stream of delivery men walked them up the front steps.

Emma had died of leukemia. But in a five-year old's mind, I killed her. *I couldn't tell anyone! No one must know! I'll be left all alone! No one will want me! God, noooo!*

I had buried the memory deep in my subconscious mind, where the guilt would forever plague me. That is, until the day at the dojo, when Patrick was able to comfort me. He told about a nasty childhood prank that he had played on someone. And, later in life, that same man committed suicide. I was not alone. I longed to find my own harmony by finding out why I was a bully as a child.

Later that evening, I journaled:

7:13 P.M. -*I am so upset. I was trying to swallow it with shopping and sugar. Bill was hollering while he worked on a shelf. I got so angry. I was so angry. That's what it was that I was burying. I was an angry child. I couldn't figure out why I was so angry. Then Sally cat and Jupiter were showing me love, and I realized what it was. As a child, I wanted to be loved and wanted. I wasn't shown that. They were not showing me love with their constant arguments. Dr. Andrews said if you hold a baby's legs from moving, they will scream in anger. Who was I angry at, my parents, or was it at myself for not being lovable? I see how I took it out on my peers. Then, that one unfortunate day, I took it out on Emma. I understand now.*

CHAPTER 44

The Rape

2005

The seasons were changing, and I was seated in Brad's recliner listening to his litany to put me deep into trance. However, something happened to me. It was real life, not Marie, as with Dr. Andrews.

In trance, I was taken by surprise.

"Mommy, mommy," I cried out through my tears.

But it wasn't mom this time. I traveled back in time to 1968: my sixteenth birthday.

"No, No!" I cried out. Schatz and I were "making out" like teenagers do. But my boyfriend didn't stop, maybe he couldn't. It was date rape. Since that winter night, I relived that day repeatedly. And now in a hypnotic trance with Brad, it came up like vomit again.

After he brought me out of my hypnotic state, Brad wanted to talk about what happened to me in trance. I couldn't, I evaded his questions diplomatically, but he was insistent. And so, I told him the story.

1967-1968

I first met Schatz on September 23, 1967, at the beginning of my tenth-grade year. I remember that day as if it were yesterday. There he was, standing with his friends in an alley when we caught each other's eye. It was love at first sight. I saw my dad in him; blonde curly hair and a broken leg caused him to limp like my father.

My girlfriend wanted to help things along with the two of us. She arranged a Halloween party that October. Schatz and I sat on the floor when our eyes locked, and he kissed me for the first time.

Schatz and I became quite an item. He was two years older than me, and we attended different schools. We always sat together on the school bus. He must have worked somewhere because he bought a shiny new silver Plymouth Barracuda. It was a wild courtship. I was a child, but he aroused a woman's feelings in me. He began to pressure me to "go all the way."

He declared, "Our friends do it all the time."

I was firm, "No, absolutely not!"

I was adamant about preserving my virginity. It was all mine and precious, I was a romantic.

It was the night of my sixteenth birthday, and I was to spend it with Schatz at a friend's house. He had other plans that night. He took me to a grassy knoll behind St. Mark's Catholic Church, one minute we were kissing, and the next minute he raped me.

I called out for mom. God, I needed her more than ever.

Schatz walked me home in silence that night. I went into my Aunt Theresa's house. She and Aunt Rose lived in the houses next to ours. I wanted to talk to my aunt. But instead, I told no one and said nothing.

After that day, Schatz and I had sex every chance we could. We were an on and off item for the next couple of years. Sex didn't stop with him. Since I had nothing more to lose, there were others. I said, "No," every time. I guess my "no" meant nothing to anyone.

That one horrible night in 1968 altered the course of my life forever. Yes, Schatz "started my dress on fire." I never dealt with my promiscuity, but it would continue to haunt me for most of my life. *God, I need to heal because I feel the pain of "sixteen" every single day.*

After my rendition to Brad, he sensed my agitation and discomfort talking to him about this sensitive topic, so the next appointment with him, he took me to "my special place" in trance. I went anywhere I wanted to go in my mind. I chose a secluded green wooded area by a pond with a double waterfall. Brad also gave me a spiritual advisor who I could call up at any time. I chose Dr. Andrews, who had passed away in 2004 to be my spiritual advisor. That wise man made such an impression on me, and he would continue to live on in my subconscious mind. When I needed spiritual advice and assistance, he would appear to me on the bench my mind placed by the calming waters in my own self-hypnotic trance. I continue to take advantage of my spiritual advisor whenever I need him.

CHAPTER 45

The Reprimand

2006

I was a smoking machine. I couldn't quit; so much pain. *I'll quit on Monday. I'll stop on Saturday—no Sunday.* Those feeble attempts never worked out. Oh, I had a million excuses; a fight with Bill, a party tomorrow night. Sometimes I made it until after lunch and sometimes supper. But really, I just never made it!

Well, the day finally came when my cigarette habit caused me a serious problem.

My office leased two floors in the insurance tower, which was in the center of downtown. I can't blame the building owners, but they were adamant that their employees didn't smoke in front of the building. They did have a spot for smokers in the back of the building. There was a little yellow square in the loading dock area where I had to smell the exhaust of the delivery vehicles that pulled up two feet away from me. Why should they care? After all, I was inhaling smoke. I couldn't "enjoy" that nicotine fix while inhaling exhaust fumes. *God, didn't they know I didn't do this because I wanted to anymore?*

I might have overlooked the "yellow block" conditions if the insurance company allowed you to walk through the inside of the building to go outside. But no, I had to walk the city block in all kinds of weather to arrive at the hole they wanted to hide me in.

Well, I had none of it! As far as I was concerned, it was a public sidewalk, and I would smoke where I pleased out there. And, I didn't work for that damn insurance company anyway. I worked for the federal government.

One day I sat on the bench outside of City Hall, which was next to our building. Along came Judge Sweitzer. She gave me the dirtiest look.

Judge Sweitzer and Ms. Tina were still out to get me, and now they had a reason. I wasn't smoking in the little yellow square. Shortly after that, I was called into the supervisor's office and presented with a letter reprimanding me for smoking in front of City Hall. I had to sign it, and they placed it in my personnel file. I was "written up."

I would not stand for it. They could not tell me that I can't smoke on a public sidewalk. I stood up for myself and called the EEOC to file another complaint. *I'll be damned!*

Well, I bet the regional office had a time with that one. A couple of days later, the supervisor handed the letter back to me while I was at the copy machine. Nothing was said. She simply handed it to me. I rescinded the EEO complaint, but I knew I had to get serious about my cigarette addiction. It was a problem.

I came to rely on Brad more than ever now. Dr. Andrews once said, find the reason for the habit, and it will extinguish itself. *I will heal my soul. I will heal.*

CHAPTER 46

Unwanted

October 3, 2006

"I have no interest in you anymore." That's what Bill had told me when he came home from the club the night before. *God, I don't know if I can make it through this one.* He didn't want me. The pain was intense. *Thank God I have an appointment with Brad today. I truly need his help.* But I didn't tell Brad what Bill had said to me after all. I couldn't tell him that I was unworthy of love. I had to hide it from people. More so, I hid it from myself.

But hypnosis betrayed me that day. After Brad induced deep sleep, my mind went back in time.

1956

Once again, I was a child, a little girl sitting on the maroon velvet sofa in the parlor. Mom placed a bowl of mashed potatoes and carrots on top of a plaid kitchen towel on the arm of the couch. She wanted me to eat lunch. I just stared at it.

"She poisoned it!" I confessed my deepest thoughts to Brad in trance.

I just knew it. To my horror, mom spoke up.

"What do you think—I poisoned it?"

I did think that, and now she said it.

She wanted me to eat, but I couldn't eat. She got mad. She told me to get out and that she didn't want me anymore. I could not move, and she left.

Still under hypnosis, I cried to Brad, "Mommy left me. She doesn't want me."

Finally, I got up and went into the corner of her bedroom, where I fell asleep until dad came home.

I ventured out of my safe place. I wanted to go outside, but I was afraid mom wouldn't let me back in. Feeling alone and unwanted, I went into the parlor and sat on the couch. Mom came in and turned the television on.

It was time to come out of the trance. The horrible memory was over, and I was relieved to be returned to a conscious state. But my relief was short-lived. I was on my way home to Bill. *God, what will it be tonight? What trauma awaits me at home?*

CHAPTER 47

The Need to Matter

March 2007

What will today bring? The thought crossed my mind every day as I headed down Main Street on my way home from work. But I wasn't prepared for the shock that awaited me. My cousin, Christopher, sought a political appointment in the April primary election. His opponent's placards lined our yard. *What was Bill thinking? He knows my young cousin is running an election campaign against this man. Why were his signs there?*

I was quite animated when Bill walked in the door.

"Who put those signs there?" I questioned Bill. I couldn't imagine who would do that to me.

"My cousin Carl put them there." Bill retorted. "I told him he could."

"Bill, Christopher is running against this man for state representative. You must tell your cousin he can't put those signs there. Christopher asked me if he could put his own signs up there, and I told him, of course, he could."

"What did your cousin ever do for you?" Bill quipped.

I was dizzy. I didn't matter once again. It was his family who wanted the signs of someone we didn't even know in our yard. Yet they knew that Christopher is my cousin. Most of the time, his family shunned me at their family gatherings. This time they really were giving me the middle finger. The worst part was that I believed them. I thought that I didn't matter.

Every fiber of my being wanted to take those signs down, but I froze. *Bill will come home from the club drunk tonight. I am afraid because he can be violent.* Sometimes I pretended to be asleep to avoid him.

To make matters worse, the next day was to be my last appointment with Brad. He was moving to Baltimore. I needed to make the most out of my final trance with him.

CHAPTER 48

Goodbyes

April 2007

My next, and last appointment with Brad arrived too quickly. I was going to miss him. We worked so well together with hypnosis. I brought him a going away gift, a small statue of the archangel, St. Uriel. His name means "Fire of God."

Brad gave me a gift, too. He made a recording of his smoking cessation hypnosis for me to use.

After exchanging pleasantries, we wasted no time getting down to business.

"I feel terrible," I stated, "I binged on chocolate. I am smoking more."

Brad said, "Your subconscious wants you to make a decision."

"I must let go of the child, Brad," I said. "If I don't quit smoking, I will never fulfill my dream of writing a book. That is the reality."

"Julija, I'm going to try something different today. Today you will free associate, and I will instruct you to remember what you saw. Then you will go home and write it.

And so, Brad took me deep into trance.

I immediately went to my special place in this rested state of mind. My inner advisor appeared. The next half hour I spent in a daydream. I let my thoughts flow like the calming waters of a brook in springtime. All too soon, the trance was over. Another chapter of my life was closing. Brad and I hugged. I glumly walked out of the office. It was sad saying goodbye to Brad and that familiar room where so much of my life was revealed to me. I took comfort in knowing that Saint Uriel was with him. My little statue would grace his new office.

Once home, I was anxious to write all the things I remembered from my trance with Brad. I got a soda out of the refrigerator, a bag of chips, and my journal book. After devouring half a bag of the salty treasure, I wrote.

PSYCHOTHERAPY WITH BRAD MITCHEL, MSW, LCSW

APRIL 2007

Today my inner advisor appeared to me as a golden orange tongue of flame. What caught my attention is that this flame did not flicker like the light of a candle. No, it remained unchanging. Feeling peace and free to speak, I told my adviser of my problem. I do not want to quit smoking. I cannot quit. I knew that if I am in the daily struggle, I will not follow my heart. I will not go outside the boundaries I placed on myself, my life. And that includes the book—the book that every worldly tragedy tugs at me to write. The spirit, once again, shows me impermanence. I see the past the same as today. The same as tomorrow will be. I have limited myself to four years old. Mommy told me to eat the food. I couldn't. She told me to get out—she didn't want me anymore. Frozen, I could not move. If I leave the house now, she will never— no, never—let me in again. She walked out the door. I was alone, and in my mind, unwanted. Why didn't I just eat?

"Why?" My inner advisor interjected to the adult, the fifty-five-year-old.

"I could not eat. There was too much turmoil in this home." I said.

I felt pain, like the flames that took the past life of Marie Antoinette Chambre.

"Was she real?" I questioned.

"Did you not feel her fear? Did you not see through her eyes as she looked at the intense orange sun of the new day breaking above the buildings along that cobblestone street?"

My inner advisor directed me to see the problem as an image now. It became the long nose of the distorted cat figurine bookends I so often gazed upon hypnotically as the cigarette smoke billowed up, up into nothingness. The limiting trance—the sameness was the problem. Day after day, it was idleness of the self-imposed boundaries.

I then became the problem. Watching myself, I needed to regulate myself. Attuned to the least little bit of change. Smoking still—more, I was afraid of the twinges of nicotine leaving my body. Yes, that's it, I realized now. I am afraid of change. I need the familiar, even if it imposes boundaries. I looked at the problem again. I see a nose. This time, it is my nose.

The flame leaves me with these words of advice, "Be like the wind. Be like the wind."

And so, I wrote the encrypted words of my final trance with Brad. Thankfully, Brad had directed me to a new therapist. His name was Dr. Adam Graincer, and he used hypnosis as a therapy tool as well. One door closed, and another opened.

CHAPTER 49

The New Therapist

July 14, 2007

I had just come home from the beach, and unfortunately, also from a "trip" into the psychotic realm of bipolar mania. I still was feeling "up" when I went to the address on Lance Street. It was my first appointment with Adam, my new psychologist.

"You have luggage with you today," Adam quipped when he procured me from the reception area.

I was carrying my sizeable beachy purse with goldfish printed on the blue canvas. It was one of my many shore purchases that year. I was manic with unlimited funds that did not exist—a financial disaster of mania. But I met Adam, and he put a smile on my face with his observation of my lovely new acquisition. The little jovial exchange bonded me with him immediately. He also had a doctorate in psychology as well. I respected that and loved smart men. *Yes, we were going to be a match!*

After we exchanged pertinent information, I went into my lamentations.

"I feel like I need to smoke for my survival," I told Adam. "But I am killing myself by smoking. There is no reason that the fear to survive should keep me smoking."

Adam interjected, "Julija, you just said you are killing yourself by smoking. How can the need to smoke for survival be a truth then?"

"Survival is in a non-smoker," I heard myself say it. The thought struck a chord in my subconscious mind and was a truth I accepted at the core. It was a spark of awareness and emotional healing about a significant challenge I would face in the coming years.

At the end of our session together, Adam told me that his plan was to get me healthy.

I felt a tinge of rebellion at that. I don't know why. Perhaps it was my resistance to change or to someone "trying" to change me.

Adam and I agreed on the date for my next appointment, which I eagerly awaited. I looked forward to resuming hypnosis once again.

CHAPTER 50

The "Devil Dance"

July 26, 2007

I was playing a game—a game like I played as a child. It was "Ring Around the Rosie"—but it wasn't. No, I was in a stupor with others circling the floor. Bill was there. We just walked in a circle—round and round in that circle with no beginning and no end. It felt evil. I didn't like the feeling. But there was no way out.

And then I sat straight up in bed. It was a dream. But the lousy feeling lingered when I woke up. In my dream, I was in what I called the "devil dance." Should I call Adam? For now, I decided to call up my inner advisor.

I took a seat in the small recliner that mom gave to us. I noticed my breathing, deep inhalations, then exhaling. Relaxed. The water gently trickled over the falls. The grass was a deep velvet green. I was in my special place, relaxed. My spiritual adviser was seated on the bench next to me.

I opined to him, "I hate myself, and I cannot stand smoking anymore. I'm not cleaning or even washing the dishes. It's just an endless neurotic freeze. I remembered telling Bill that he had to break the pattern and quit drinking for a day. Well, I must break the pattern too. It is becoming too painful for me to smoke."

I felt my spiritual adviser with me. I opened my mind to him. I heard him say, "Bill will continue to have drunken incidents. The feral cats will still overwhelm you. You'll have to deal with mom and with work. Life will go on the same whether you smoke or don't smoke. You cannot use those things as an excuse to keep smoking anymore."

I saw that I'd find new ways to cope. Maybe it would be easier if I was feeling better physically and psychologically.

The next couple of days, I was in and out of my own personal debate. I felt the "sickness" of the nicotine leaving my body. I was restless, dizzy, and the days felt long. I'd want to smoke one day and promise myself I'd quit the next. Therefore, I was neurotically sick when I didn't smoke and tried to stop, and I hated myself and only thought of quitting when I did smoke.

It's all about an addictive weed. It's the devil dance, and there is only one way out of it. It wasn't a matter of finishing a pack of cigarettes or making sure I had a pack with me at all times in case something happened. It was not just saying "I quit" without even thinking of the horrible withdrawal I would feel followed by the first twinges of panic because I didn't feel normal. Of course, I won't feel normal. My body hadn't been normal since I was fifteen.

I remember sewing the burgundy sport coat that I made for Bill before we were married. I had just vowed to the Mother of God to quit smoking for one month. I was starting to sew the coat, and I said to myself, *I shouldn't have stopped smoking now because I wanted to take a sewing break and smoke a cigarette.*" and then, *Well, I'm not smoking.* That was the end of it. I simply continued working on the coat and moved forward without a cigarette.

Bill was wearing a burgundy sport coat in my devil dance dream. There is only one thing that will break the cycle. I had to get out of the vicious circle I saw in my dream.

CHAPTER 51

Cold Turkey

July 27, 2007

TGIF—thank goodness it's Friday, I thought, as I walked around the block to the side of the insurance building. I now had a little nook between pillars where I stood to smoke. It was out-of-the-way from sidewalk traffic except for the insurance employees walking to the small yellow block in the loading dock.

One day, Santa Claus stopped by. I wasn't psychotic! A jolly looking man with white hair and beard stopped to talk to me.

"You are really enjoying that cigarette!" He noticed cheerfully.

He knew that I really was not "enjoying" my smoke break. It must have shown. And then I began to look at other people smoking. They had pain written all over their faces too.

Before the man left, he said, "Try the patch. It really works."

Then he added, "Ho! Ho! Ho! I'm Santa Claus!"

And now I think that maybe he was because the weekend had arrived, and change was in the wind!

July 29, 2007

I woke up and decided to finish my pack of cigarettes and then quit smoking. The thought of being without cigarettes scares me. But if Bill comes home crawling on his hands and knees, having that weed doesn't change anything. It doesn't mean anything if I have a cigarette or not. I will do whatever I have to do to move forward. I think I can see that now. Maybe for the first time. I quit smoking at 9:15 AM on July 29, 2007.

12:15 PM, and I'm positive about the quit attempt. I just want my body to heal now.

At three o'clock, I had finally made it back from the laundromat without smoking, even though something happened that upset me. A lady took my finished wash out of the machine while I was out in the car, waiting for it to run through the wash cycle. That had never happened to me before. It wasn't as if the laundry sat in the machine for a long time. In fact, it probably just finished. I was right outside in my car. If I was smoking, it would have made me go back out to the car and chain smoke. So, what the cigarette does is give me something to do while the anger or fear passes. Not smoking, I felt it and let it pass.

When Bill comes home falling down drunk, I would sit there and smoke the bad feelings away. So, I was doing something while the emotions pass, especially when I had absolutely no control over the situation. Smoking numbed me to the emotional pain by stifling those feelings instead of allowing myself to feel them. But the bad feelings are not a constant ten on a scale of one to ten. They do pass. When the lady took my wash out of the machine, I felt insulted. However, I did handle it well. I thanked her for her help. My feelings were an eight. But when I am masking the feelings by smoking, they are still there. I simply do not acknowledge them. That's all. But they are still there.

I was well on my way to making it through day one of my cold turkey attempt!

CHAPTER 52

Withdrawal

August 1, 2007

Day three. Every muscle was pulled like a guitar string ready to pop. But I moved forward. My chest ached. *Is it my lungs missing the deep inhalations of smoke that used to invade them? Perhaps they're healing. But I am moving forward.* That morning at work, I couldn't sit still for five minutes. Finally, I gave up! I just gave up!

I fumbled through my purse for my cigarette lighter and slipped it into my slacks pocket with a $10 bill. *I'm going to the newsstand for a nicotine fix. I'm buying a pack of cigarettes.* Going down the elevator to the lobby, I counted the floors, five, four, three, two, one. Something happened when I reached the lobby. I never ran in my life. I'm not a runner. Lord, I hadn't exercised since 1993. But a calm came over me. Instead of going to the newsstand, I ran two blocks to the river. Then I ran back to my office. I moved forward through with a fuzzy mind. Withdrawal was a bitch.

After supper, I sought the escape of sleep. I was in physical and emotional pain. When sleep came, I still felt the intensity of the anguish. My mind moved through the suffering like waves on the sea. Coming and going. I rolled with the power of it as if I were in a trance. Coming and going. That was my life for a while.

Then three months passed. I felt better, although there were times of weakness. Bipolar depression reared its ugly head. Sensei told me it was because little strands of neurotransmitters were dying off from the lack of nicotine that put them there in the first place. During the past several months, I had relied on him. And more so, I relied on Adam and his valuable talent for hypnosis. While waiting for the doctor, I memorized the paintings in Adam's reception room. I even took pictures of them and of that room. I memorized it, every chair, every lamp. And when the pain was most unbearable, I studied those pictures almost hypnotically. That practice generated some relief to get through the worst of the pain. I hung onto Adam's every word of encouragement.

Maybe I was going to make it, after all. Seasons came, fall, winter, spring. And then I celebrated July 29, 2008. One year! I credit my success to all my doctors and counselors. But especially to my gift for hypnosis. Maybe I could finally be free.

CHAPTER 53

The Accommodation

February 21, 2014

I walked three blocks to the Blue Door Restaurant at lunch. Finally, it was my last day at work. My manager had planned my retirement luncheon. No one else would do it. I could not have stayed there any longer. I barely made it to age sixty-two, which gave me twenty years of service.

I was surprised to see the vocational experts and judges at my party. My friends were not there because they were afraid of Judy, the leader of the old-school clique.

I regret getting so caught up in that clique. It happened so innocently, but it was devastating to me.

It all began in 2000 when I became a legal clerk and moved to the rear of the office. I sat in an adjoining cubicle with Judy. Oh, how easy it was to get caught up in that clique. We sat close to each other, and I thought she really liked me. The truth is Judy was a user. I thought I was special and cool to be included. I was a member of the "gang." After all, Judy accepted me, and she was the unofficial leader.

Judy played the anti-management role, but she secretly bought the supervisor, Peggy, gifts. I saw the teddy bear in Peggy's office with a card from Judy. When it came time for Recognition Awards, Judy always got one.

In the meantime, I kept being called into the supervisor's office because my work wasn't moving fast enough, or my numbers were too low. It was always something. I was always the one being badgered. And while this was going on, Peggy was having sexual relations in her large corner office during overtime hours with Clyde, a fellow legal clerk. He showed the lewd pictures she had sent to him to everyone who would look at them. It was dirty.

Then came the time for reviews. Judy came through with flying colors. In fact, she got the highest score you could get guaranteeing another thousand-dollar award. I barely passed. I saw what was happening. I had learned from A Corp. I was going to stand up for myself. I had enough.

Due to my anxiety and bipolar disabilities, I went through the usual channels for an official request for accommodation. I asked for three fewer judges to schedule hearings for. It would help get my numbers up. My request was accepted by the central office.

I told no one, but Judy didn't miss anything. She watched me and counted my hearing days. My dear friend filed a union grievance to find out why I had fewer judges. She went around the office, alerting my coworkers to my accommodation. She sat at her desk, making nasty comments about me. She was turning my friends against me, and she was the girl who used to tell me she loved me. As it turns out, she didn't know what love really was.

For years, she had worked at home, and she told me that she never even took her cases out of her car trunk. She completed them while in the office. I never told anyone. She cheated in the sign-in book, as she clocked in at an earlier time than she actually arrived at work. And, she stole from the supply room to spite the clerk in charge because she was mad at her. But Judy was the leader of the pack, and everyone was afraid of her. Even management gave me the three hardest judges to work for every single month instead of rotating me like everyone else. I asked the lead clerk if it was a management directive.

She said, "You could say that." I knew it was all done to appease Judy.

Well, the last straw was when Judy drew my dear friend, Nikki, into her fold. I sat at my computer, afraid to move. I was a scared five-year-old child again sitting alone on the couch.

It was time to move my desk. I sent off an email to management. I was being bullied, and I requested they move me to the other end of the office.

Judy put on such a crying act the day of the move. Although at the time, I did fall for it. I kept apologizing. She cried to everyone. She had to make it look as if she were the victim. Well, being on the "outs" with this ringleader made me second fiddle to my friends. They still had to work there, and I was retiring. They told me as much.

I said before, my friends did not come to my luncheon, but I know now, my "true" friends were there. They were friends who were not click material in Judy's eyes. I had been such a fool as Judy's follower all along; not my own person. That was over, I had put in my twenty years, and I was free. *But was I really? I had so much to work through emotionally. I had to find out who I was.*

PART II

POST-RETIREMENT

CHAPTER 54

The Nightmare

2014

I never felt good because, for some reason, I could not let go of the past. It tormented me; during my waking hours, it's a neurosis. *What is wrong with me? Why do people hate me? They can't hate me!* I had never questioned this before. I simply believed that I deserved the bad treatment I so often received. I just accepted it. *Now that I am questioning myself, is it a sign of a new beginning in my quest for peace of mind? Maybe I am ready to open my mind to the valuable awareness's which I seek. And possibly, with Adam's help in hypnosis today, I can expose the subconscious source of my suffering in a trance.*

It was a Saturday morning appointment per usual. After Adam and I exchanged pleasantries, I wasted no time recounting the nightmare that frequently awakened me from a fitful sleep.

"In my dream, I'm a child again," I told Adam. "The back door is locked. I stand alone on the concrete porch. The door appears larger-than-life, but it's locked. Mom and dad locked me out of the house. They didn't want me, so I stood there alone. And then I wake up!"

My heart pounded as I recalled the details of the nightmare to Adam.

"Would you like to do hypnosis, Julija?" Adam asked.

I nodded eagerly, "I need to know."

Adam turned the lights down, and I took to the recliner. Listening to his mellow voice quickly put me into a deep sleep. I focused on that locked back door, and soon a memory surfaced.

I told Adam this story while in trance:

"My cousin, Marilyn, and I are playing with our majorette dolls that grand-mom bought for us. I can recall their every detail from the braided blonde hair to the white and gold satin dresses they wore. Aunt Rose, who lived next door to me, called for Marilyn to come inside. I was now alone in her yard. Then I spotted it. She left her doll on the lawn chair. Now is my chance. I grabbed the doll and ran. I ran to the exposed sewer pipe in my backyard. I stuffed the doll down the pipe. I pushed it down with a tree limb I had found on the ground until it was no longer visible.

The next thing I knew, I was in the living room.

Mom was yelling at me, "Now I have to give Marilyn your doll," she threatened.

I saw myself, and I saw my mom holding my doll. I saw both of us as if watching a movie. There was more, but my subconscious would not release it to me. I was too scared.

And so, Adam gave me a time of silence where I could contemplate what I felt. I didn't understand it, but I felt fear for my very survival.

Well anyway, it was a beginning, but I needed more. Somehow, I knew it just wasn't time yet. However, I was stubborn, and I was not giving up! I would get the answers I so desperately needed.

CHAPTER 55

The Broken Hip

June 25, 2016

My retirement years were passing by so quickly. It seems like I took the first several years just to recuperate from the past forty years of working. Unfortunately, I still suffered from bouts of psychosis. This one proved detrimental to my mother.

It was all my fault. Mom had fallen, and I sat in an emergency room far from home. God, I did it. I wanted to kill myself. I never felt so strongly suicidal. Finally, my brother, Mike, came to sit with me beside her bed. He had followed the ambulance there. He was angry and not talking to me. *It's my fault this happened, and he knows it.* My only recourse was to take my life.

The doctor came into the room with the verdict. My ninety-four-year-old mother's hip was broken, and she needed surgery.

We were 100 miles from home at my dear nephew's wedding in Wilkes-Barre. I had been psychotic–dancing to rock and roll wildly with mom. She loved to dance. I took a spin, and she wouldn't let go of my hand. We both ended up on the floor, and she couldn't get up. *Please get up!* I was stunned, and as I said, I was psychotic. Out of sheer necessity, I had come back into my "right mind." We sat mom on a chair, and after a while, thankfully, Mike took charge.

"Come on," he told me. "We're taking her to the hospital," Mike called an ambulance and arranged with building security for a wheelchair. Thank God for Mike that night.

When the doctor said mom needed surgery, I finally stepped up to the plate.

"No, we are taking her to the Hershey Medical Center for surgery," I stated.

I was insistent. We needed to be there for her during her recovery. We couldn't stay in Wilkes-Barre.

So, the hospital arranged for her ambulance ride home. It was a long night, so I was thankful when Bill came to the hospital to retrieve me. I don't remember the rest of the night and the long ride home.

The next morning, I was at the medical center to meet the ambulance and my mother. She was glad to see me, her caregiver. I took her everywhere with me until dementia made it too difficult for her to go out.

She had been failing and should never have lived alone for as long as she did. A couple of months ago, I had to crawl into the kitchen window to help her. She had fallen getting out of bed, and I had a hell of a time picking her up. I took her to the emergency room then, too. It was a bad experience. This old woman with dementia sat in the waiting room for four hours before we finally left without her even being seen. We both were exhausted from the ordeal.

Surgery at the medical center was scheduled for the next morning, but mom was "out of it" mentally.

"What is Theresa doing standing there looking at me?" Mom quizzed.

Aunt Theresa had died years before. *What did mom see that we didn't? Where did her broken mind take her?*

Surgery the next day was a success. Afterward, we needed to put mom in a nursing facility for physical therapy. Catherine wanted to keep her at home with caregivers, but that was not viable financially. And more so for me, I could not do it anymore.

I was mentally exhausted from going to her house every day to get her up and dressed and make sure she ate. And then there was always the dread of her leaving the stove on or somehow hurting herself. It was too much.

After Catherine and I spent the day visiting high-end facilities, we finally settled for the more practical Lutheran nursing home in the neighboring Township. It was not as elegant as other residences we toured, but the staff took exceptional care of my mother. However, even with physical therapy, mom never walked again. It was a downhill slide from here.

Catherine, Mike, and his lovely wife, Anna, visited mom every day. Anna took the morning shift. I was there for noon Mass that was broadcast on EWTN TV, Mike was there in the late afternoon after work, and Catherine was there in the evening. But mom was declining. She had to eat mush as she couldn't swallow, and her liquids had to be thickened. It was hard for us to watch this.

She clapped when I arrived for my visit because she was so happy to see me. She would want to go with me whenever it was time for me to leave.

"I have to pick Bill up," I would appease her. "Then I'll be back for you."

"Are you sure?" she asked every time.

"Yes," I assured her, "I'll be back for you. You wait here for me."

And everything would be repeated daily. That's the way it went for the next six months until January 2017.

CHAPTER 56

End of an Era

January 4, 2017

Who would have known at mom's ninety-fifth birthday party in the recreation room of the nursing facility, she would die nine days later? It doesn't seem right. She wanted to dance as Joey, a family friend, played polka music for her on his accordion. Of course, she couldn't even stand since she had broken her hip six months prior.

I will never forget the look of death in mom's eyes that January day. Her beautiful sky-blue eyes appeared blackened, glazed over in a blank stare as she opened them when the nurses shifted her position in bed. It was getting late in the day, and my brother and sister had to leave. Mom and I were alone. I put EWTN on TV. It's the Catholic station mom, and I had watched over the past several months at the nursing home. She liked to watch Mass, and it comforted me. I was glad for this time alone with my mother. I laid my head on her warm shoulder as she lay there, awaiting her passage. I cried as my head rose and fell with each labored breath.

I told mom, "I know I wasn't always good. But I turned out okay, didn't I?"

I felt that my mom somehow heard me. I believe she was aware of my sobs. On TV, they were singing "Joy to the World" at the end of the Mass.

It reminded me of the record mom bought me when I was a child, "Joy to the World," with a beautiful angel printed on the vinyl.

And then the home's Lutheran Pastor came in to say a prayer for mom, "Yea though I walk through the valley of the shadow of death, I will fear no evil."

It was a comfort to me, as well. I had a horrific migraine. I wanted to be with her when she died, but I couldn't stay any longer.

Choked up, I said my goodbyes, "I'll be back for you, mom," as I always had to say to appease her when she wanted to leave with me. This time though, I knew I was leaving for the last time. My sister called me at two o'clock in the morning. I knew what Catherine was going to tell me when the telephone rang, "Mom died."

The end of an era. God, I miss that woman. I gave mom three white roses to hold in her hands while she lay at rest in the funeral parlor. I also put my Sacred Heart scapular from childhood into her hands. It had a special meaning for me.

I had been fortunate to have Adam as my psychologist since 2007. I still treasure every visit with him. He is an influential person in my life who helped me to achieve much awareness, which freed me of suffering. He wrote a sympathy note to my family when my mother passed.

A short note to offer you and yours heartfelt condolences on your mom's passing. I know you have struggled and experienced ambivalence in your complicated relationship with her. However, recently, you seem to have more resolve and to your credit, forgiveness toward her.

Ambivalence—I looked the word up in the dictionary. It is the coexistence within an individual of positive and negative feelings toward the same person, object, or action, simultaneously drawing him or her in opposite directions.

Ambivalence causes much conflict and guilt. I realized I had been ambivalent to my mom for a long time, fluctuating between love and hate for her. How can a person hate their mother? Unfortunately, it wasn't until after her death I realized she was a person. I needed to see my mom as a human being, a real person with pain and suffering of her own, not some godlike perfect being or a "paper doll" like the cutouts I played with as a child.

February 28, 2017

I see the neurosis that is my feelings for mom as a child—witch or mommy. I see the confusion it created inside of me—the ether mask—going round and round. I see the ambivalence. I can see it, and I see my fear of it. It's one thing to say it or be told it, but quite another to have the awareness. It is my fear she will "find out" that I believed her to be a witch. She was an adult with anger issues—not a witch. I feel the neurosis. It is from childhood. I don't have to fear it. I can feel it now.

I remember saying to mom once when I got mad at her, "I don't like you."

And she said, "You never did."

That destroyed me. I'm sorry I didn't like you. She felt the same way about her mom. I see that is how she "knew." That is, it! She knew what I was feeling about her because she felt the same way about her mom. And that is the awareness that soothes my neurosis.

CHAPTER 57

The Helpless Child

April 13, 2017

Dr. Sandra, my Psychiatric nurse, told me to take care of myself. She said it must be nice to hold your mother in your heart. I see myself letting go of the past and embracing the future. Dr. Sandra mentioned my history of being abused. And now I know that I didn't want to admit I have been abused because I believed it was my fault. God, that awareness just hit me. Deep down inside, I believed I deserved to be beaten. I can finally see I believed it to be my fault. I got awareness. I believe the way I was treated was my fault. Oh God, I see the helpless child. God. It came up from my subconscious. Oh, mom, I know you didn't mean it. My love for you is unconditional. But I feel anger at you right now. Oh God, I was only a child. I believed I was evil. God. How did I survive? I see my life passing by. God, I could cry now, but I'm going out to get my nails done, and I don't want my mascara to run.

April 17, 2017

My problem now is knowing I survived. It is PTSD, and I need the awareness that I did indeed survive the abuse of three years old. I know it consciously; but, more importantly, I need my subconscious to register that I survived.

I hoped Adam could help. I sat in my car and waited for the clock to tick down the minutes to my appointment. Finally, it was time to walk up the three flights of steps to my dear friend and advisor's office. We exchanged pleasantries, and I told Adam of my predicament. We agreed that a hypnosis session might help me solve the quest for awareness.

Adam talked me into a relaxed state of mind with his soft-spoken words. I prayed to mom to be with me as I entered my subconscious. I came up as a three-year-old again. Mom was slapping my face. *How many times have I relived this moment?* I still needed to resolve it. Maybe I never would, after all, that is what PTSD is.

While in trance, I relayed my feelings to Adam. I was quickly caught up in the story that unfolded.

I was three again. I desperately pleaded in my dream-like state, "I can't be me. I can't be me. I can't be me!" I exclaimed in horrific pain.

"I killed my 'self.'" I cried. "I can't be me who this is happening to?"

In desperation, "I killed my 'self.'"

I needed Adam to understand. My "self" was my sheer essence, my being, my soul. I needed to escape even while in a trance. I left my body just as I did back then.

"Outside" of my body, I told Adam that I saw our neighbor lady at the screen door. I remembered seeing her in the yellow light emanating from the outside fixture.

"You didn't have to beat her," she admonished my mom.

I told Adam about her putting the cold towel on my forehead. He asked me if I felt safe with the neighbor.

I replied, "No."

Voices commanded me, "Go back. Go back."

"Who told you to go back?"

"God." I replied.

"I see a light." I was coming back into my frail little body.

As Adam brought me back to the present time and out of the hypnotic trance, I found myself taking deep breaths and heavy sighs. I had to hear and feel myself breathe. It's amazing! I felt mom's spirit holding my hand when I went into my trance because I was scared. I subconsciously knew what was going to transpire. I prayed. It was challenging to recall.

One day in her later years, I got mad at mom when I was dyeing her hair in her kitchen. I don't even remember why, but I told her in the heat of an argument that I remembered how she kept slapping my face when I was a child.

She cried out, "I can't live with that. I'm going to kill myself!"

I feel bad about that now. She had dementia then and was anguished. I see where I got the word juxtaposition. I had to kill my "self" (who I was) because I could not be a helpless child with no way out. When I brought it up to mom in her later years, she said she was going to kill herself because of the guilt and anguish of that memory. Quite a juxtaposition.

Adam told me that I could let myself be human and have human emotions. I was always afraid to feel because I always felt fear.

April 18, 2017

I feel great love for my mom right now — God, mom, what you lived with. Thanks for helping me yesterday. I'm feeling pretty proud of myself for all the work I have done. And I feel peace.

CHAPTER 58

Frozen in the Past

April 20, 2017

It has been over twenty-five years since A Corp, but I still cannot accept what happened to me there. I wondered if I had multiple personalities. The whole A Corp affair was a flashback to three years old. But it was more than a post-traumatic stress disorder flashback. *Thank God Adam was able to squeeze me in today. I need to hear myself think.*

Seated across from my therapist, I told him of an article I read on the internet regarding the psychological fight, flight, and freeze response. I was caught up with the freeze response, the inability to fight back or flee the situation.

"I understand there was nothing else I could do at age three." I reasoned. "My mom's anger overcame me. She held me there by my arm and just kept slapping my face. I couldn't breathe. I couldn't run. She had me by the arm. There was nothing I could do but leave my body. Subconsciously, I took a snapshot of the trauma, and that part of my 'self' froze in time. Do you follow what I'm trying to say?" I asked Adam.

"Yes," Adam responded. He went on, "The last hypnosis session we did, you said, 'I can't be me. I can't be who I am.' What was happening then?" Adam prompted.

"Well, I see where I completely disowned my 'self' at three. I completely denied three to be a part of my 'self.' You know, Adam, that part of me broke off."

Adam continued, "Then when you broke off, who were you? Who did the three-year-old become?"

I thought for a moment, "Three became the phobic person. The person with shaking hands."

"How ironic," Adam replied. "The phobias were so you wouldn't have to be three and helpless again. But with the phobias and psychosis, you were helpless to control yourself once again."

"I think I see what happened at A Corp," I explained. "It was a flashback that brought out the frozen three-year-old. It was controlling Sheila and authoritative Elwood. I couldn't alienate Elwood. Somewhere inside of my broken mind, I needed that man, the father figure, for my survival. And controlling Sheila, my mother figure, was turning him against me. I was helpless once again. It was three, and mom was saying, "Don't tell dad. He won't like you. Thank you so much, Adam. I see it now. I understand."

We set up my next appointment after this successful session was over. It was another awareness realized. I was growing up. I was well on my way to seeing who I was!

CHAPTER 59

I Was Her!

August 2017

"It took hours to get to this hotel in the country. I have no idea where it is located. For some reason, I'm furious at the owner. And there are huge bugs all over this place. I tore out the pages in my journal book and threw them on the floor in anger. I have to get out of here. I want to go home."

I wrung my hands as I explained last night's dream to Adam.

"Go on," Adam encouraged me.

"Well, I found a way out of the hotel with a group of men and women going to a fast-food restaurant. They all piled into a tan van."

"Funny thing about this," I noted, "the van was just like Bill's van, and one of the men was a credit manager I worked with at A Corp."

I continued, "We stopped at a gas station, and when I came out of the restroom, I saw the van going down the road. They left without me. I tried to run after them, but I was left all alone.

"Adam," I said, "I can feel my insecurity. I was in this strange place and had no idea where it was."

"Julija," Adam asked, "do you want to do hypnosis on this?"

I was terribly upset but agreed to this session if only to relax me.

Adam talked me into a trance with his usual calming voice. He gave me time to work out this fear in a relaxed state. I saw myself as a five-year-old child.

1957

"Oh, no!" fear took hold of me. *"There's something wrong with dad's car!"* I cried in my mind.

Dad yelled at mom, "You just had to go to Hershey, didn't you?" He was angry.

He is hollering at my mommy! She remained frozen in the front seat. She and I are scared. Dad pulled over to the side of the road as a cloud of steam poured out of the engine.

I'm not safe! Nooooo! Please! I want my home.

Dad blamed mom, but he may as well have yelled at me too, for, at that moment, I was her. I identified with my mother. We were somehow bonded.

Adam spoke once again after giving me time to process my fears.

"Were you able to find your answer to what will help you today?" he asked.

I responded with a nod of my head. I had the beginnings of a resolution.

2017

When out of my trance, I told Adam that I felt like I was my mother. In a sense, dad was yelling at me. *Was it because I took on my mom's identity as the female figure to me?*

Adam asked, "Did you ever feel that you took on your mom's personality before?"

After a pause, "I can still see myself. I was outside on the swing with my brother. It was my 1991 psychotic break. God. I panted, and it was like I became my mother."

"You don't want to drink that soda," I commanded my little nephew. "It will make your mouth sticky." I was her. I was her domineering self.

I remember Dr. Ambrose saying to me in 1991, "You are not your mother." But for that instant, I was her. *I was her!*

"God, Adam. I need to understand."

Adam urged me on.

"Adam," I said, stunned, "I took on mom's personality at three. I couldn't be helpless. I took on the personality of the aggressor. Only after that, I bullied my peers. Then my four-year-old cousin died of leukemia."

"What do you think you felt then?" Adam asked.

"Fear," I stated. "Now, I had another horrible secret. I had to bury that part of me. I thought I killed Emma because I gave her sumac to eat. I have been petrified of anger ever since then. I couldn't let myself feel anger. *God, suppose they found out that I 'killed' her.*

And after Emma died, I went to the complete opposite end of the good/bad poles. I became abnormally 'nice.' I couldn't get angry, and everyone had to like me. But then came A Corp and my federal job…The pent-up anger became major depression."

August 20, 2017

    I am starting to see, at this moment, I am not my mom. I am my own person. Even in taking on mom's personality, I remain myself. I must see myself let go of that time of my life. You know, she was mean sometimes. I went the complete opposite way. I see where I went to the extreme of being nice—so so nice. And I wouldn't let myself get angry. But now I see that I can get angry without hurting anyone physically. I was so afraid of anger. In my eyes, it was a sin. And it was either her or me—myself. That is my neurosis. That always has been the fight! God, I see. I just felt three. I felt the horror of myself—a child. God, no wonder I couldn't be me. God, I feel it—heavy sigh. I took her on. I feel my insecurity with people. I feel the neurosis now. God, it's the struggle to maintain me.

    I walked and tried to convince myself that I am my own person. It was a neurosis. I see what happened at three. But I am now an adult. I see I am my own person. I am an adult. I understand now.

CHAPTER 60

Revealing the "Secret"

October 2017

I waited patiently along the road for Bill's cousin's wife, Jennifer, to come by for me.

Jennifer and I hit it off right from the start when we were introduced in 1970. But more so recently, in the past several years, when we began to compare notes about our dysfunctional in-laws.

For so long, I believed it was only me. But she experienced shunning by their illustrious family matriarchs as well! I wish Jen and I had that conversation earlier in our relationship. I had gone through so much with my in-laws for most of my married years.

However, that was a sad day for us. We were going to visit Jen's niece and Bill's cousin, Cathy, who had melanoma.

Cathy was in her forties and had been fighting cancer for the past five years. She was one of the family who always treated me like a regular person, not some creature with five heads. That is the way that Bill's family always made me feel. Things certainly had changed in the past couple of years. Maybe it was because I had stopped trying to be accepted by them. I gave up.

But Cathy was always so kind, And Jennifer and I planned to visit her that morning.

Jennifer arrived, and she and I chatted away, exchanging family news and gossip. I'm sure that we sounded like two little old women talking "over the fence."

Finally, we arrived at Cathy's house. Cathy was in the living room, seated on a large recliner. Her sister, Lisa, was in the living room with her. Cathy was sobbing when we walked in the door. She had just come from the oncologist who had been treating her with immunotherapy. The cancer was in her lungs; however, therapy failed to stop cancer's progression. That morning, the doctors had told her there was no more that they could do for her.

"I have to fight this cancer!" Cathy sobbed.

I saw at that instant her realization that she was dying. *God, how could this happen?* She was only forty-four years old.

It was one of those moments when you are not quite sure what to do. And so, I decided to tell her my Medjugorje story.

"Cathy, I want to tell you a special story. I have told very few people about what happened to me during my trip to Medjugorje in 1988. I tried to tell your grandma years back, but I was rudely interrupted before I could tell of the miracle." I commenced.

"It was a Thursday night during my pilgrimage to Medjugorje. I stood outside of St. James Church because there was no room inside. Suddenly the clouds scurried rapidly. And then I saw this figure in the clouds."

"I cried because I was so afraid. I was in awe, and I couldn't look directly up at her. She began to pat my hair down because I was so scared."

"'Don't be afraid,' she soothed me."

"'Who are you?' I asked insistently. 'Who are you? I must know.'"

"'I am the Mother of God,' she responded."

"She talked to me and told me of things. But then the vision began to fade away."

"I said, 'Are you leaving me?'"

"'I will always be with you,' she assured me."

"And now, Cathy," I said. "She is with you."

Jennifer and Cathy's sister, Lisa, left the room. Cathy and I were alone. I went over to her and patted her soft brown hair.

"Don't be afraid," I comforted her.

"I am," she cried.

But in her voice, I heard the beginnings of acceptance.

Finally, after all these years, I got to tell my story of the Medjugorje miracle. I only hoped that Jennifer and Lisa didn't judge me too harshly for telling Cathy.

But for now, my thoughts and prayers went out to Cathy and her family.

CHAPTER 61

The Shunning

The ride home after leaving Cathy was especially solemn for us.

Jennifer broke the silence, "So who stopped you from telling your Medjugorje story to my mother-in-law all those years back?"

I told Jennifer my story, "I wanted so badly to be a part of Bill's family when I married him. You know that I held his family in high esteem, especially his father and mother. I did have mental issues. However, I hid it well. There were times when I felt especially vulnerable, and to be around, his mom and dad made me feel safe. Maybe that's why it hurt me so much the day Bill's dad shunned me. It wasn't only his dad, some others in the family shunned me as well."

"I know what you mean," Jennifer chimed in. "My sister-in-law does it to me all the time. Please continue what you were telling me," she urged me on.

"In 1991, I was deep in bipolar psychosis. I always had a hard time letting go of the pain when his family dissed me. That was because it meant so much to me to be accepted by them. I felt I needed his family for my very survival."

"Well, it must have been a holiday when we were visiting Bill's sister, Martha. I was on the sofa with your mother-in-law and her friend, another older woman named Barb. I loved your mother-in-law (who was Bill's, Aunt Veronica). She always treated me like a regular person. In other words, she didn't shun me like so many in Bill's family did. She reminded me of my own dear aunts. Well, I proceeded to tell the ladies of my paranormal experience in Medjugorje, and I was cut off in mid-sentence."

"'How are you, Barb?' Bill's dad yelled across the room in his Eastern European language to Aunt Veronica's friend sitting next to me. I knew it was intentional because of the tone in his voice. I was destroyed and felt worthless. I guess I can understand why he did that. In his eyes, I was an insane embarrassment."

"Julija, you could never be an embarrassment in my eyes!" Jennifer assured. "But go on."

"Unfortunately," I continued. "That incident and others with the family caused me to completely reject their nationality and anything associated with it. The thing is, it was my heritage as well. But Jennifer, you see how it was Bill's family's passionate identity. Everything had to be Eastern European music, flags, and shields. I stereotyped them with all that was Eastern European. I never revealed my anger at them. I was always gracious. But that is what it became, anger at a nationality, my own heritage. I couldn't help it."

Jennifer pulled up to my driveway, and we said our good-byes. The whole day left me completely drained. I hoped Bill didn't expect a big supper.

CHAPTER 62

The Childhood Vision

2017

I became neurotic. *Why did I tell Cathy, Jennifer, and Lisa, the story of the Medjugorje miracle? God, it's going to get all around now. What will people think of me? No good will come of it.* All I could visualize was an incident that occurred when I was about seven years old. My mind took me to that warm summer day in 1959 at 6732 Hilltop Avenue, my childhood home.

1959

I frequented our neighbor's backyard. Marsha, Rich, and I played together almost every day. They had the most wonderful butterfly tree in their yard. Today I was on my own standing in front of the tree's majestic purple flowers. I smelled the freshness of the breeze emanating from the woods below. Everything was right. And then I spotted the flutter of orange wings on one of the branches. There it was!

Slowly my fingers approached a "Queen," a beautiful monarch butterfly. I caught it!

"Let go of the butterfly," the lady in the bush commanded.

Immediately my fingers obeyed. I released the "Queen."

"Who are you?" I questioned the beautiful lady.

"I'm your Mother," she replied.

"No," I was confused, "My mom is down there." I pointed to my house next door.

"I'm your Mother in heaven."

"Will I go to heaven when I die?" I asked.

"Yes," she replied.

She told me of things that I cannot remember, but I had the excitement of a child. I *had* to tell someone. *I must tell mom!*

"I have to go home now," I repeated anxiously to the magnificent vision of the lady in the bush. "I have to go home. My mom is looking for me."

"Mom, mom," I burst through the kitchen door, "I saw the Blessed Mother in the butterfly tree!"

Mom was not pleased. "Don't say that!" She admonished me. "God will punish you."

I was so disheartened at mom's negative response.

My mind returned to the present time. But the memory left me as disheartened as I was when I was a child. I was afraid of telling the truth back then, and I still was.

CHAPTER 63

Last Respects

November 2017

This can't be good, I thought as I rode by Cathy's house and saw the lineup of cars parked there. Sure enough, early the next morning, Jennifer was on the phone.

"Cathy died at nine o'clock last night," she reported.

Cathy remained foremost on my mind the next couple of days. She was cremated and was to be buried on top of her mother, who died a year earlier. But first came the evening viewing service at the local funeral parlor in Milltown.

When Bill and I arrived at Windhim's Funeral Home, the line of people to pay respects wound all around the outside of the building. We waited an hour just to get inside the doors.

Cathy was a grade-schoolteacher, and it struck me how her colleagues tearfully hugged each other mourning their loss.

When inside, I saw the picture boards that lined the hallway to the main room. It was pictures of Cathy with her family, my husband's family, that choked me up.

Cathy had an incredible regular life. She was a teacher and had so many friends and was so loved. She had her family, and she was accepted. She was involved in her community. She was everything I wasn't—couldn't be. I wept for my life of suffering and mental illness. Cathy was cremated, but I could feel her presence there. I felt her. She was at peace.

The next morning at the funeral mass in church, her family and friends played the Eastern European stringed music for her. They sang the songs. I felt terrible about that. I was not accepted by Bill's family in those early years of my marriage. I needed their approval, but they mocked me. I needed an acknowledgment that I was someone. That I am. But in their pain, they couldn't do that for me. And as Adam had schooled me, I realized then that it was their own schema that I took upon myself.

Now "schema," as Adam said, is the "box" we put what happens around us into to make sense of our own world.

Finally, I saw that those women in Bill's family perceived me as some kind of threat to their own "selves." That is why they were so ignorant to me when I was only kind to them. It was their own pain, their schema, that I was taking upon myself. And it was my schema that I was not worthy of love that perpetuated the suffering for me.

Several days following the services, I walked up the road to the cemetery where Cathy was buried. I plucked a dried rose from the bouquet that had surrounded the urn holding her ashes at the funeral parlor. She was at peace. I still have a hard time accepting my pain, but I am working hard for the peace of mind I so embrace. And now, every time I'm at the kitchen sink, I look at that dried rose on the windowsill, and I remember Cathy.

CHAPTER 64

The Bishop

January 1991

"Father Silva is on his way up to your house now," my sister-in-law's voice on the telephone line sent me into a downward spiral. My whole body shook, my heart raced, and I felt like I was being pursued by a mad dog. Death was imminent. At least that's the way I felt.

But it was only St. Bernard's priest stopping by to bless our house for the new year that threw me into a major panic attack. It was January 1991, and I had been psychotic for a whole year by then.

Suddenly, I heard the person who "dwelled" in my mind speak.

"Go to the sliding glass door," the voice inside my head beckoned me. "Now breathe on the window," he went on.

My breath on the glass appeared as a fog. "See your breath," the voice urged.

I kept breathing on that pane. Seeing my own breath was calming me. The panic was subsiding. I was graciously able to receive this priest into my home.

2018

That is the way it was for much of my life, panic attacks, phobias, a flurry of irrational daytime "nightmares" for me. Now, due to psychotropic medication, I have been relieved of those constant panic attacks.

However, even with the medication, my bipolar mania sometimes flared up. A spring manic episode surfaced once again. Unfortunately, it was the day of the celebration mass and reception for Bishop Gabriel on his twenty-fifth anniversary of ordination into the priesthood. Before becoming a bishop and moving to a parish in western Pennsylvania, he was my parish priest at St. Bernard's.

I remember this Bishop for his enthusiastic hugs when he was our parish priest. However, I felt a special bond with him the day I was a patient at the hospital recovering from a psychotic episode in 1996. I sat on the bench in front of the hospital, taking a smoke break on that warm spring day. Father Gabriel came walking by. It was so good to see a priest. Just talking to him back then gave me great peace. Priests were always special to me. Dad instilled that philosophy in me because of his priest friends who had been so good to him.

I was glad when my dear friend Elizabeth joined me for the festivities. The mass was as beautiful as I anticipated it would be. And after we sang the last song, I had Elizabeth wait as I scurried back to my car for the Bishop's gift.

Earlier in the day, I had wrapped the special present with great care. I tucked black-and-white monogrammed napkins into the gold foil bag in place of tissue paper. I was so excited.

Well, as I said, I was manic. And, walking to my car, I ran right into Bishop Gabriel as he was leaving the church. I gave him an enthusiastic hug.

In my mania, I squealed with delight, "I love you!"

Well, I retrieved the gift bag in the trunk of my car, and Elizabeth and I proceeded into the church hall for the party. I couldn't wait to give the Bishop his gift.

Elizabeth and I chatted away as I watched Bishop Gabriel go from table to table, expressing his cordialities. Our table was next, and I was like a child giving a gift to her father. But alas, he walked right by us without stopping.

I did not hesitate but to jump up and go after him.

"Bishop Gabriel," I addressed him, "I have a present for you. I hope it's alright. I was manic when I bought it."

"I'm sure it will be fine," he replied.

"I was hoping we could sometimes talk," I told him. "You know, I saw the Aseity of God."

He replied, "Yes, we'll talk." And then he proceeded to bless me with the sign of the cross.

And with that blessing, I felt the painful dismissal that was so familiar to me. I knew he didn't take me seriously. And I knew it was because I was mentally ill.

It wasn't the first time I was dismissed by a holy man. Several months earlier, I had asked Father Robert, St. Bernard's parish priest, if I could talk to him.

He said, "Yes, we'll talk." I realize now that the only reason he agreed to talk to me was my name and nationality. You see, my husband's family were the prominent "protesters" when the different nationality churches consolidated. He simply was trying to appease a protester. But I was not a protester.

When my appointment to see Father Robert at the Diocesan Center arrived, I was psychotic once again. Unfortunately, in my mania, I only spoke the truth. I confessed to him that I was manic, but what I told him was important. After all, it is true that young people are leaving the church. I proceeded to tell him why.

The meeting only lasted fifteen minutes. And when I tried to make another appointment, I was shunned once again.

"There is no one who can talk to you," the priest left the message on my answering machine.

Now, I am done with priests. *I'm sorry, dad. I'm just done.*

I got out my pen and paper, and in anger, I wrote.

Dear Father Robert and Bishop Gabriel,

I'm sorry that I was psychotic when I tried to make conversation with you, and more importantly, I wanted to make friends with you. I am sorry. But what I told you back then was the truth. And I'm not psychotic now. You see, from the tragedy that was "3," I had a problem speaking the truth, especially when it was "politically incorrect." I'm sure you can understand that. I regretted what I told you both back then. But today, I do have disappointment. It is in how you dealt with me—a person in pain. You see Bishop Gabriel, because of the church "scandal," you were "afraid" of me when I hugged you outside the church and animatedly said to you, "I love you." But I did Bishop Gabriel. I did—and only as a person—not a lover. I asked you to talk to me. I was so excited when you said, "We'll talk." You didn't even send me a thank you card for the gifts I had to go out of my way to give you because you avoided speaking to me at the social. I'm sure you saw the gift bag sitting on the table in front of me when you visited every table but mine. You were afraid. For God's sake, we were in a church hall! And Father Robert, you only agreed to an appointment with me because you believed I was one of those "displaced" St. Bernard's protesters. Well, I wasn't, and, once again, I was psychotic on the day of my meeting with you at the Diocesan Center. But I spoke the truth to you. The Catholic Church is losing young people. And I did talk to Buddhist priests and now wished to speak to a Catholic priest.

Do you know Father Robert, that once when I went to see Sensei Earl, a Buddhist priest, I was psychotic?

He asked me, "What can I do for you?"

"Just talk to me," I implored him.

That day we had the most wonderful philosophical conversation. He made a person who went to him in pain feel relief for a time. Well, Father Robert, you told me your duties have changed, and you could not make future appointments with me. I asked you for a priest I could talk to—to have future appointments. You told me no one could talk to me. I am angry. Are you following my Christ? I wanted to have philosophical conversations with a man who followed my Christ. And Bishop Gabriel, did my telling you I saw the Aseity of God frighten you so much? Or was it when I told you I was manic when I picked out your gifts? And Father Robert did you "shut me off" because I told you that the Catholic Church needs to focus on man as eastern religions do, rather than focus on God. You see, people are in pain. God is not. He is God! I was in pain, and I needed my church. But you abandoned me. My old church, St. Margaret's, the one you sold because you had to pay off sex abuse victims, had and still has a picture of St. Martin on the ceiling. Perhaps you, Father Robert, and Bishop Gabriel should read up on St. Martin!

Sincerely, Julija.

When my anger was quelled, and my letter was written, I folded the paper and tucked it in the back of my journal book. I needed to walk.

CHAPTER 65

The Fear for Mike

April 2018

"It's a repetitive dream," I told Adam. "I'm hiding below the windowsill at mom's house, and I know someone is peering into the window above. I press my body closer against the wall so that whoever it is can't see me. I'm too frightened to look."

I took a deep breath and continued telling Adam about the recurring dream. "Well, finally, last night, I did. I looked to see who it was. I felt intense fear when I saw my brother, Mike's distorted face pressed against the glass pane. It was my brother! It was Mike who appeared in the window."

"You seem perplexed," Adam chimed in.

"I don't know why I would be so afraid of my brother," I replied.

"Can we do hypnosis about that dream?" I asked Adam.

Before I knew it, I was in the recliner and in a deep hypnotic sleep.

1963

"I'm running after Mike!" I frantically told Adam while in a trance.

I was an eleven-year-old child. I saw myself turning the corner of the house.

"He's bleeding!" I exclaimed in one quick breath.

I caught up to my six-year-old brother in the driveway. Mike had plunged right through the glass window of the storm door. God, blood, and glass were everywhere. When I finally got him into the kitchen, mom was of no help. She was in utter chaos.

"Get a towel out of the drawer!" I coaxed mom as I held onto Mike. Thank heavens, the neighbor came to help. We didn't have a telephone back then.

"Go next-door and get Uncle Jim to take Mike to the doctor!" I directed my panicked mother.

Aunt Theresa must have found out that something was going on next door as she came running in the door.

"Mary," she said to my mom. "Get your coat on. Jim will take you to Dr. Bernstein's office."

They all left, and I was alone with blood everywhere. I was so afraid for Mike. I don't want to lose my brother.

"God, please save Mike," I silently begged in extreme distress.

Mom had a statue of Christ, the Infant of Prague statue that sat on the parlor windowsill. I swiped Mike's blood off the kitchen floor with my finger. I transferred the blood to the raised hand on the infant's statue. And then I heard Mike in my mind, *Jules, Jules!*

Immediately, the fear for Mike's life left me. *Mike's okay, Mike's okay!* I was so relieved and calmed.

Adam was confused. "Where was Mike when you heard him call you?"

"At the doctor!" I exclaimed as if Adam should have already known that. I heard Mike call me in my mind. God had answered my prayers.

"You took care of everything even as a child," Adam said half to himself as he awakened me from my hypnotic sleep.

Once awake, I told Adam, "What was so eerie about that day was that when everyone came home, Aunt Theresa told me that Mike kept calling for me as Dr. Bernstein worked on his wounds."

CHAPTER 66

Powerless

October 2018

My little white furball, Cecilia cat, had died in Bill's arms late the night before. She wasn't even sick to our knowledge. She "reported" for breakfast yesterday morning with the other three cats. God, I was going to miss my "little little" as I so dubbed her.

We brought Cecilia into our home as a critically wounded feral kitten some fourteen years ago. At that time, she had been violently attacked by an outside creature, maybe even another cat. Bill was especially fond of her. I credit him with saving her life. He diligently fed her with an eyedropper. Since she was prone to walk in circles, he taught her to walk straight.

Her death was so sudden, and now it is hard to grasp. Bill was outside, digging her grave. He was in such pain that I ignored my own and worried about him. My only comfort was knowing that I gave her a kiss last evening when she came out of her favorite hiding place under the dining room table to greet me.

Cecilia and I bonded because we both suffered from fears. We both were "attacked" early in life.

To "mask" my suffering, I reached for my old "cure-all," a bag of cookies. But as I did, I saw myself clearly. I couldn't control Cecilia's death, and I couldn't control Bill's grief. Meanwhile, I was shoving my own pain down with sugar. And not so much pain for my cat's death, but more so that I did not have everything under control. I could not control life and death or Bill's happiness. I had absolutely no control!

I was "out of control" as I shoved cookies, one after the other, into my mouth, I searched the Internet: "Hyper responsibility." I once heard Adam call it that. I "surfed" until I came across an article written by Janet Singer, "OCD and Hyper Responsibility." She wrote, "Those who suffer from hyper responsibility believe they have more control over what happens in the world than they actually do."

"In the world," resonated in my mind. I saw the expanse of my belief in those few words. I saw the extent of boundaryless control that I believed I had.

The awareness hit me! I felt my irrational belief that I needed to control everything that happened in this world. I needed to control people and how they felt. I needed to control how they felt about me. It finally hit my subconscious nerve.

I understand what I had been searching for for so long. I needed to put my newfound belief into practice. That is not as easy as it sounds. I had a goal and moved forward.

CHAPTER 67

Forgiveness

December 21, 2019

"O Come, O Come, Emmanuel," the choir sang to open the Saturday evening mass at St. Bernard's Church. The priest walked down the aisle to the altar that was strewn so beautifully with red and white poinsettias.

My mind drifted to Bill; *I hope he made it home safely. Snow squalls possible, the weatherman predicted. Bill is out in that 1941 Packard. Does it even have windshield wipers?* I always worried about him when he was out for a ride in that thing.

How can I possibly think I can control Bill's safety when I can't even control myself with shaking hands and psychosis? I admonished myself. I was drawn back into the church service by the beautiful prayers and chants.

Father Daniel's sermon commenced, "A Jewish Rabbi's wife suddenly came down with the flu. His one-year-old son was without a babysitter. The Rabbi had no choice but to take his child with him to the evening service." Father Daniel went on, "The youngster squirmed in his father's arms. He kept interrupting the Rabbi's sermon. First, the Rabbi had to rescue his necktie from the child's mouth; and then his glasses from the little boy's clutches. Perhaps the Rabbi's loving actions toward his son said more than any sermon ever could. It was obvious. The kindly father forgave the child with each disruption."

My mind drifted, and I saw why I couldn't forgive my father-in-law. He disliked me because of my mental illness. I realized that I hated myself, and I had never forgiven myself for being mentally ill. *I'm sorry, Jerry, that I was a mental case.* I prayed to forgive my father-in-law.

I was angry at myself. But then, Bill has rages and so did mom. They had a mental disorder. And what's more, dad went through psychosis in 1970. At least he was saying crazy things back then. I heard him during the night accuse mom of having an affair. Oh, how far from the truth. Yet, I forgave them in my love for them. *So why shouldn't I love myself and forgive myself for being human as well? Why should I disown myself because of my disability?* I believed that with the realization that I was only human, too, I could learn to accept myself.

CHAPTER 68

Sex Addiction

December 26, 2019

I stood in the rain at Schatz's grave. In that cemetery where my daily walk took me, I spoke freely and cried if I needed to.

"You started my dress on fire," I told his headstone through my tears. "You predetermined my life with that one evening in 1968." I went on. "From that rape, I became addicted to sex. At sixteen years old, my stomach did somersaults, and my body shook violently when I stood in line to confess to a priest that I was 'with a boy.' I was so shy. But I believed back then that it was a sin."

"God," I said as the rain dripped from my jacket hood. "And it wasn't just you, Schatz. There were others. You know, I tried to fight them off. But I now wonder, did I really? God, I couldn't stop myself. I erroneously believed that masturbation was a sin, too. God, I was only being human. But I couldn't stand myself. I made a vow to the Blessed Mother that I wouldn't do it anymore. But alas, the pull for sexual release was too great. That one night, I caved. I felt so completely evil that I hid it in the very depths of my subconscious only to surface as an unnamed searing pain. I can name it now, guilt. You did that to me, Schatz. Well, you opened the door."

I continued, "And I believed no one would want me, but I needed to have one person so that I wouldn't be with everyone. It caused me to make bad choices. There was alcoholism, rages, and psychological abuse in my life. Do you see what you did?" I asked the grave marker, a ghost from the past.

My only consolation is that my belief system had changed. My Christ was a human being. And why couldn't he have kissed Mary Magdalene on the lips as the apocryphal gospel of St. Philip stated? Why couldn't he have been married to her? He was a human man. I am only human, too.

My emotions were spent, I wiped the tears from my cheeks and walked down the street toward home. I saw the weight of that one February night in 1968. But more importantly, I saw my own humanity.

CHAPTER 69

The Family Gathering

December 28, 2019

"My cousin Tim broke my heart last night," I told Duane, my hair stylist, as I was getting a desperately needed haircut.

Duane was my friend, but more like family for the past forty years. This tall, handsome man always had a hug and kiss just for me, and especially a compliment for something mod I wore. Surely, he would understand my plight.

I continued to tell my story to him. "Last night, we had a family gathering to celebrate our moms, the Putsco girls! All six are gone now, but we are cousins. And we consider ourselves Putsco strong!"

I went on, "All of my cousins are loving and down-to-earth. They all care. All except for Tim and his sisters, Janice and Tina. There was always something that I felt from them. I knew they talked about me in an unflattering way. Was it jealousy? It may have been." I told Duane as he clipped my locks.

"You know me, Duane," I said. "I'm not one to dress conventionally. I like a little flash."

We laughed, and Duane added, "Hon, you always look nice!"

"Thanks, Duane," I said, "but last night, my cousin Tim didn't think so." I felt the hurt as I went on with my story.

"Well, I wore my new jeans with the sparkles going down the front of the legs. And I wore my sneakers with matching sparkles. Tim came into the room. He stopped dead in his tracks, stared at my slacks, and exclaimed, 'Oh my God!' He just stared at my legs."

"I looked at him and said, 'What? These?' And I pointed to my jeans. He stood there frozen, saying nothing. Then I said, 'These?' And I pointed to my sneakers. Duane, Tim just shook his head, turned around, and walked away. He made me so self-conscious. I just sat at the dining room table for the rest of the night."

I continued, "Janice was odd to me too. I feel that they have something against me. But we're family, and it shouldn't be that way."

"Hon, it wasn't you," Duane said to comfort me.

I was glad for his ear. But I needed an awareness. Thank heavens for mass later that night. Meditation always helped me.

CHAPTER 70

The Judgement

December 28, 2019

Deacon Samuel was saying mass with Father Daniel. As they proceeded down the church aisle, my mind drifted back to spring Bible study with Deacon Samuel.

I loved those Bible classes. Deacon played the DVD of a lecture, which I would rebut in my journal as I listened to the speaker. I am a bit of a rebel at heart. Don't get me wrong, I love my Christ and my religion. But I do not believe in all the rules and regulations that men have initiated.

"Any comments?" Deacon would ask the class.

I never spoke up. My beliefs are personal. But that night, on the turn of a dime, Deacon Samuel looked straight at me, "You can't pick and choose what you believe?" He scolded me.

I was taken aback. *Why did he do this?* I never spoke my opinion to anyone. I did slip up one evening and called the miracle of the loaves and fishes a parable. *Did someone tell him that? Or was someone looking over my shoulder as I journaled my remarks to the DVD discussion?*

In a slight panic, I responded to Deacon, "I thought that something is a sin only if you believe it to be a sin."

"No," both Deacon and another man retorted at the same time. "You only have to be aware that it is a sin."

"Well, Christ said to make no laws other than what are in the Torah," I remarked. And then I went on, "You cannot judge."

"You cannot judge." my mind returned to the present and to this mass I attended. *That's it!* I was so afraid of being judged. From childhood conditioning, I feared being judged.

I remembered Marilyn's majorette doll (the doll I shoved down the sewer pipe as a child). I remembered my mom yelling at me. And then, I remembered that which was so hidden from me, even in hypnosis with Adam.

Mom had said, "No one will want you! You will be all alone!" It was a moment frozen in time. As a child, being unwanted and alone meant that I would not survive.

The puzzle pieces came together. It was all falling into place. My hands shook because I feared judgment by everyone. It was why I couldn't go to communion. I couldn't walk in front of all those people judging me. *No one will want me. I will be all alone. I can't survive on my own.* I cried with relief. I found the reason for the shaking hands. *I am going to be free! I am going to be free!*

December 29, 2019

Today I got the awareness that I only need myself to survive. I didn't need Bill. I didn't need Schatz. I don't need mom and dad anymore. They needed me! They all needed me! I see, and I am angry at myself. It cost me my mental health. I needed his family. I needed the priests. I needed everyone. I am angry. Oh, at myself. But I see it so clearly now. I don't want to revert to the old ways. I will be 68 years old. I need to be healthy. I have a lot to do. I accept it! I feel peace. I am sane, and I accept working for you, my God. I accept your son in my mind—helping me—directing me. And I believe in you, my Mother of God! I accept.

CHAPTER 71

The Release

February 1, 2020

The weeks turned into a new year. 2020! I called it the year of the book! I would publish my book this year! I attended a Saturday evening mass that celebrated the Feast of the Presentation of the Lord.

In the readings, I saw myself in the second reading as the minister read Hebrews 2:14-18, "…. And free those who through fear of death had been subject to slavery all their life…."

It was me. God, how I feared for my survival all my life. I reflected on that. But then there was more. Father Daniel began his sermon, "A young bride stood at the altar with her betrothed. The bride's mother and father looked on. They are happy for their daughter today. There were so many happy days with their little girl."

"Their thoughts drifted back to her birth. She was the most beautiful baby they had ever seen with her curly blond hair. And then they remembered her first school dance with a young man. They could still see her in that blue satin dress with long white gloves. Oh, and it was her first pair of high heels, black patent leather."

As Father Daniel went on with each segment of the bride's life, I saw with great sorrow that that bride's life wasn't my life. Tears welled up in my eyes as I thought of the reading. I was always afraid as a child. I saw the dysfunction in my family. I would have been sobbing had I been alone, maybe walking through the cemetery. But I could only think of despair and darkness. *How did I survive? Tell me, why can't I move past it?* The anguish welled up in my throat, and it remained there until my car door clanked shut after mass was over.

With a flood of tears, I screamed out. I was three again and felt the intense fear that I felt back then. It raged throughout my whole being. I felt a fear I have never allowed myself to acknowledge. I saw myself as a child, my life threatened. I panted and cried as I gasped for air. I couldn't get enough air in my lungs. A little girl in so much pain.

"Hail Mary, Hail Mary," I prayed.

It was what I so needed to release, the fright I felt like that little girl being beaten. I knew it was done. All I could think of was Marie going to the fire and to her death. And perhaps that was me. But tonight, I finally spent the fear. I was free at last!

CHAPTER 72

I Wrote a Book!

February 2, 2020

The brisk air stung my face as I walked against the wind to Churchvale Cemetery. My daily exercise took me through the narrow pathways of this old neighborhood landmark.

Although I felt a remnant of childhood fear that morning, it was leaving me. It was being replaced with a renewed joy for life. Yes, things were different for me since my awareness the night before. There was a spring in my step, and I was smiling. I even heard a flock of geese flying on their migration north, a bit early in the season, but an indication of upcoming spring. It always amazed me how their instinct guided them.

As I finally reached my destination, my mind took me to the book chapter that I was currently working on, Bishop Gabriel's 25th-anniversary celebration. Dismayed, I remembered being psychotic that day. I thought of my bipolar disorder and how it couldn't be cured. It could only be managed with medication. And when I "fell" to mania and depression, all I could do was pick myself up, dust myself off, and keep moving forward.

I had just passed Schatz's tombstone and turned the corner of the tar path on my way home when I froze! The orange sun peeked through a dark gray opening in the winter sky. Suddenly, Joy filled my heart. I laughed, and I cried. I saw what I had done. I took my life of mental illness, my own experiences, and I dissected them, piece by piece, awareness by awareness. In amazement, I thought, *I wrote a book! I did that! I wrote a book!* Now, perhaps my life of tribulations can help others who suffer as I did.

And then it struck me! *Dad, dad, when I had a vision of you that one day in 1986, you told me that I would be happy! Dad, I really saw you! You are still there—somewhere there! It was you!* I never trusted in my visions before. But way back then, in 1986, no one could have known that I would ever be happy, especially me. *But dad, I am very happy!*

The End

EPILOGUE

A winged bird flew across the sun
Feathers shown crimson fire
His path was endless though
I wonder where the angels lead him.

To eternity or just the end of time minds live on.
Tears being shed or maybe just
drunk from the heart
Gentle bird glides across the sun.

Torn between hatred to feel for a brother
Happiness for the newborn's cry
Sorrow for the man who died
Fly high for a while or maybe forever.

Blinded from view in the vast clouds
But wiser than man who perceives
Images of other man in hate.
Lonely despair is what one can't feel
if he's born in the air or not born at all.

Lightning struck a heart of stone
It lives on but the stronger
Terrified and starving thoughts change the world
My mind desperately grasping for wisdom or death.

The bird rested; death was mine.
My heart, my mind, my soul
Life is all around, but my heart only beats
for the bird whose journey has ended.

by
Julija Rudolf
1968

MENTAL HEALTH ASSISTANCE

Substance Abuse and Mental Health Services
Administration (SAMHSA)
www.samhsa.gov
www.findtreatment.samhsa.gov

Suicide Prevention Lifeline
1-800-273-TALK (8255)

National Helpline
1-800-662-HELP (4357)

Veterans Crisis Line
1-800-273-8255 and press 1

American Society of Clinical Hypnosis (ASCH)
140 N. Bloomingdale Road
Bloomingdale, IL 60108
www.asch.net
(630)980-4740
Email (info@asch.net)

Printed in the United States
By Bookmasters